CARLOS ALBERTO SIESQUEN SANDOVAL
CARLOS ALBERTO RIOS CAMPOS
HENRRY WILFREDO AGREDA CERNA

BUSINESS INTELLIGENCE SOLUTION

CARLOS ALBERTO SIESQUEN SANDOVAL
CARLOS ALBERTO RIOS CAMPOS
HENRRY WILFREDO AGREDA CERNA

BUSINESS INTELLIGENCE SOLUTION

TO MANAGE THE EXPENDITURE OF A FINANCIAL INSTITUTION IN NORTHERN PERU

ScienciaScripts

Imprint

Any brand names and product names mentioned in this book are subject to trademark, brand or patent protection and are trademarks or registered trademarks of their respective holders. The use of brand names, product names, common names, trade names, product descriptions etc. even without a particular marking in this work is in no way to be construed to mean that such names may be regarded as unrestricted in respect of trademark and brand protection legislation and could thus be used by anyone.

Cover image: www.ingimage.com

This book is a translation from the original published under ISBN 978-3-8417-6832-2.

Publisher:
Sciencia Scripts
is a trademark of
International Book Market Service Ltd., member of OmniScriptum Publishing Group
17 Meldrum Street, Beau Bassin 71504, Mauritius
Printed at: see last page
ISBN: 978-620-3-36270-1

SUMMARY

This research consists of providing a business intelligence solution in a financial institution, whose purpose of the implementation of the solution is to contribute to the process of making appropriate decisions to improve the analysis of expenditure management.

For this solution, various business intelligence development methodologies were reviewed, both traditional and mixed, as well as current trends; obtaining a proposal with the following phases: Analysis of information requirements, Business Model, Analysis, Design, Construction and Implementation.

As a tool for the Business Intelligence solution, the Pentaho Suite was used in the Community version under the OSBI (Open Source Business Intelligence) scheme.

The solution provides decision-makers with the ability to set guidelines for expense accounts based on the possibility of quick analysis.

Keywords: *Business Intelligence Solution, Decision Making, Business Model, Information Requirements Analysis, Expenditure Management.*

TABLE OF CONTENTS

INTRODUCTION

The objective of this research project is to develop a business intelligence solution that can help senior management to make intelligent decisions and maintain competitiveness in the microfinance business.

Today, many managers face the paradox that "they have more and more information and less and less time to analyse it".

This solution should display the information required for the analysis of the expenditure item in a time-saving and user-friendly format, thus providing a tangible benefit, which can provide a competitive advantage to decision-makers.

The paper will describe the implementation of a Business Intelligence Solution for Expense Management applied in a Financial Institution.

CHAPTER I

PROBLEM STATEMENT

1.1 PROBLEM DESCRIPTION

One of the central objectives of financial institutions as private companies is to maximise profitability, and to this end, one of the variables to be controlled is expenditure.

Currently, the financial institutions, which are the object of this research, have transactional systems in which their daily operations are recorded. Their main transactional core processes the information of their main operations, such as their Savings and Placement or credit business processes.

The administrative Core, also called ERP (Enterprise Resource Planning), records the daily administrative transactions and provides us with information about them. Here, the expenses that are produced in the different Agencies, Offices and/or Stores, as well as the organisational and functional units that the institution has, are recorded, according to what is kept in the accounts of the expense item. In this regard, there is information that has been produced over several years in the different expenditure items.

However, we do not have a tool or solution that allows us to analyse this information historically, by our management indicators, by time period, organisational unit, cost centre, geography, functional hierarchy and classified by items or trends to help senior management make decisions in this regard. Currently, many managers face the paradox that "they have more and more information and less and less time to analyse it".

This tool should display the information required for analysis in a format appropriate for strategic level users in a timely manner. A format similar to pivot tables, with the ability to obtain graphs to allow them to efficiently and effectively analyse expenditures.

This information provides senior management with the possibility to make better management decisions or set guidelines for expense accounts, based on the possibility of faster analysis.

1.2 PROBLEM FORMULATION

Does a business intelligence solution, through the Pentaho Suite, contribute to the analysis of expenses in a financial institution in Piura?

1.3 RESEARCH OBJECTIVES

1.3.1 GENERAL OBJECTIVE

Implement a business intelligence solution, using the Pentaho Suite, to analyse expenditure management.

1.3.2 SPECIFIC OBJECTIVES

1. Formulate and consolidate information through management indicators to measure expenditure management.

2. Design the necessary dimensions to perform the Multidimensional Analysis of the solution.

3. Use tools from the Pentaho Suite for ETL processes, such as Pentaho Data Integration (PDI), under the use of Data Integration - Kettle.

4. Build a data warehouse - DataWareHouse, with Pentaho tools, to perform Multidimensional Analysis or Online Analytical Processing (OLAP).

5. Deploy the business intelligence solution model, with the artefacts generated from the Pentaho suite.

1.4 HYPOTHESIS

The development of a business intelligence solution will contribute to the analysis of expenditure management in a financial institution.

OPERATIONALISATION.

Identification of Variables.

<u>Dependent Variable</u>: Improved Expenditure Management, in a financial institution.   <u>Independent   Variable</u>: Business intelligence solution.

Scoreboard.

ITEM	VARIABLE	INDICATOR	CONCEPT DEFINITION	OPERATIONAL DEFINITION	UNIT OF MEASUREMENT	MEASUREMENT TECHNIQUE	MEASURING INSTRUMENT
1	Improvement in the management of expenditure in a financial institution.	Follow-up and control of the Financial Institution's Annual Operational Plan	Expenditures executed, in the monthly, bimonthly, quarterly, quarterly or annual time period in the financial institution.	$$PGEPPR = \frac{\sum_1^n MEPP * 100}{MGPP}$$ PGEPP=Percentage of expenditure incurred by item per period. MEPP=Money Executed per Item per period. MGPP= Amount of total expenditure incurred for the activity per period.	Percentage Currency Currency	Inspection of records. Data processing using dimensional analysis tools.	Database, which stores information on expenditure incurred by item in the various periods.
	Improvement in the management of expenditure in a financial institution.	Average unit cost per expenditure incurred	Total average total expenditure for an activity for which expenditure has been incurred.	$$CPGR = \frac{\sum_1^n CATG}{NATG}$$ CPGR=Average per expenditure incurred. CATG=Cost of the activity. NATG= Number of activities that had expenditure.	Currency	Inspection of registers	Database, which stores information on expenditure incurred.
	Business intelligence solution		This is the average time it takes to generate a historical expense report.	It is controlled with a stopwatch, obtaining the average.	Weather	Direct operation	Stopwatch and Observation sheet N° 01.

		Time taken to generate a historical expense report.		$$TPGR = \frac{\sum_1^n TGR}{N^0 R}$$ TPGR: Average time to generate a report. TGR: Time taken to generate the report. NR: Number of reports.			

1.5 METHODOLOGY

1.5.1 TYPE OF RESEARCH

Research is of the applied type, which is characterised by the fact that it seeks the application or use of the knowledge acquired.

The use of Business Intelligence tools, such as Multidimensional Analysis, will be applied.

Applied research is closely linked to basic research, as it depends on the results and advances of the latter. Moreover, it is an activity whose purpose is the search for and consolidation of knowledge, and the application of knowledge for the enrichment of the cultural and scientific heritage, as well as the production of technology at the service of the country's integral development.

Level of research: Descriptive and applied.

Descriptive studies seek to specify the important properties of individuals, groups, communities or any other phenomenon under analysis. They measure or evaluate various aspects, dimensions or components of the phenomenon or phenomena to be investigated. Hernández et al.

1.5.2 RESEARCH DESIGN

The design of this research will be Descriptive, Non-experimental. For Briones, longitudinal means that data is obtained from the same population at different times during a given period.

1.5.3 POPULATION

The population will be delimited by the data from the analysis of the financial institution's expenditure, but on information from 2014 - 2016.

1.5.4 SAMPLE

The population sample, corresponding to the present research, will be composed of the entire population.

1.5.5 DATA COLLECTION TECHNIQUES

The data collection techniques used are: direct observation, documentary and archival data analysis.

1.5.6 INTERPRETATION OF DATA AND/OR RESULTS

For this research, the information will be analysed, processed and reviewed with data analysis tools, but above all with the use of descriptive statistical analysis tools, supported by the observation sheet.

1.6 RATIONALE AND IMPORTANCE OF THE RESEARCH

1.6.1 JUSTIFICATION

This research is academically justified because it allows contributing with knowledge, providing the use of tools that support decision making, which is characterised by the shared

use of a Business Intelligence (BI) solution, with the Pentaho
Suite, which is an Open Source Business Intelligence tool.

This research is socially justified because it reduces time in
obtaining information and resources in the decision-making
process, allowing them to make a quick and effective
multidimensional analysis of expenditures.

The use of Business Intelligence tools, such as the Pentaho
Suite, will help in the decision making of senior management, with
the use of multidimensional analysis of information.

1.6.2 IMPORTANCE

This research provides us with the use of technology, under
an adequate business strategy, with well-defined processes; it
generates the transformation of data into information and this in
turn into knowledge; to correctly analyse the various items of
expenditure and optimising them.

It will provide a deeper understanding of the various
methodologies and tools for the development and management
of Business Intelligence Projects.

CHAPTER II

INSTITUTIONAL, LEGAL, THEORETICAL AND BACKGROUND FRAMEWORK

2.1 Institutional Framework

One of the central objectives of financial institutions as private companies is to maximise profitability, and to this end, one of the variables to be controlled is expenditure.

2.2 The Cajas Municipales

In May 1980, Decree Law No. 23039 was enacted, regulating the creation and operation of municipal savings and credit cooperatives outside Lima and Callao, with the aim of building decentralised financial institutions targeting those segments of the population that had no access to the formal credit system.

Since the creation of the first Caja Municipal de Ahorro y Crédito in 1982, the CMAC System has positioned itself as a fundamental element in the financial decentralisation and democratisation of credit in Peru, giving various social sectors access to credit and encouraging savings, contributing to the creation of local financial circuits, which are the basis of support for the regional productive process, while becoming the leaders in microfinance.

In this context, the first Caja Municipal de Ahorro y Crédito was founded in Piura in 1982 with the support of the German Technical Cooperation, whose financial experts contributed to the design of a growth strategy for the Cajas Municipales de Ahorro y Crédito in Peru.

Law No. 27602, "Ley General del Sistema Financiero y del Sistema de Seguros y Orgánica de Superintendencia de Banca y Seguros", establishes the regulatory and supervisory framework to which companies operating in the Financial and Insurance System, as well as those carrying out activities related or complementary to the corporate purpose of such persons, are subject.

2.3 Scientific Theoretical Basis

2.3.1 Information System (IS)

The Information System of an Organisation is that part of any organisation that is formally dedicated to capture, store and transmit relevant and pertinent information for the Organisation to all the members of the Organisation, so that they can carry out the activities entrusted to them, as well as exchange information of interest to the same Organisation with other people or organisations. (Lluis Cano, 2007).

Figure 1. Information System Components.

Source: (Lluis Cano, 2007)

2.3.2 Business Intelligence (BI) system

Business Intelligence is to sustainably and continuously support organisations to improve their competitiveness by providing the information necessary for decision making. The first to coin the term was Howard Dresner who, when he was a consultant at Gartner, popularised Business Intelligence or BI as an umbrella term to describe a set of concepts and methods to improve decision making, using information about what has happened (facts). Through the use of Business Intelligence technologies and methodologies we aim to convert data into information and from the information we are able to discover knowledge. BI is an interactive process to explore and analyse structured information about an area (usually stored in a

DataWareHouse), to discover trends or patterns, from which to derive ideas and draw conclusions. The Business Intelligence process includes communicating findings and making changes. Areas include customers, suppliers, products, services and competitors. (Lluis Cano, 2007).

Benefits that can be obtained through the use of Business Intelligence (BI):

- Tangible benefits, e.g. cost reduction, revenue generation, time reduction for different business activities.
- Intangible benefits: the fact that we have the information available for decision making will lead to more users using this information to make decisions and improve our competitive position.
- Strategic benefits: All those that facilitate the formulation of strategy, i.e. which customers, markets or products to target. (Lluis Cano, 2007).

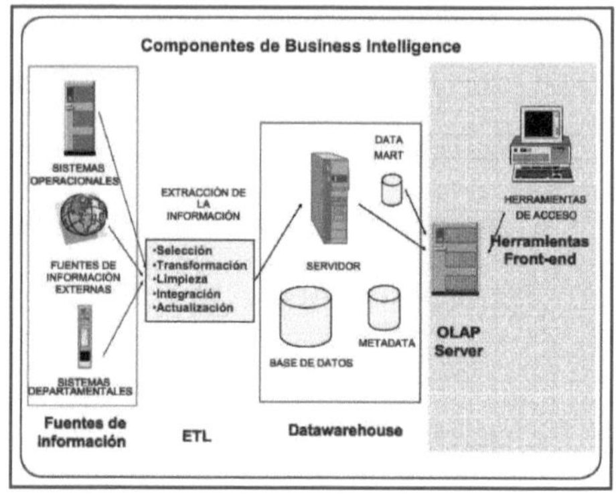

Figure 2. BI components.

Source: (Lluis Cano, 2007)

2.3. 3 Business Intelligence Methodology

Among the BI methodologies, the best known and most widespread is the Kimball Methodology, called the dimensional business lifecycle, as shown in this image. (kimball & Caserta, 2004).

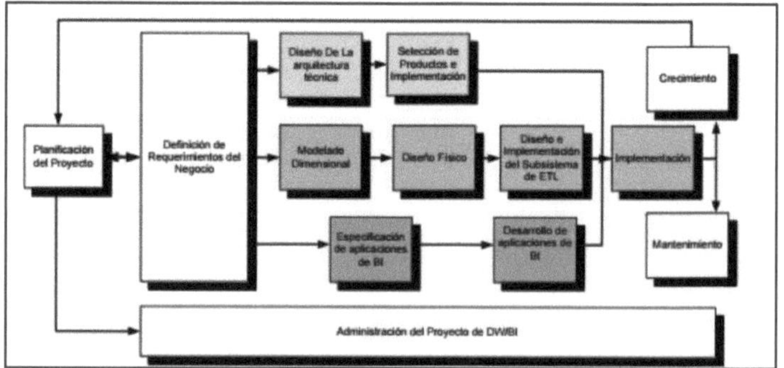

Figure 3. Kimball Methodology Tasks.

Source: (kimball & Caserta, 2004).

2.3.4 Pentaho

It is one of the most complete and mature suites on the OSBI (Open Source Business Intelligence) market and has been in existence since 2006. There are two versions: Community and Enterprise. It is composed of different engines included in the Pentaho server:

- Reporting: supports static, parametric and ad hoc reporting.
- Analytics: supports OLAP (via Mondrian) and data mining (via Weka).
- Dashboards: using CDF (Community Dashboard Framework).
- ETL: using the Kettle tool.
- Metada: which provides an information access layer based on business language.
- Workflow: the Pentaho server is based on actions that most business objects allow you to launch.

Currently Pentaho follows the Open Core strategy, from an Open Source core, services and enhanced modules are offered, which is why there are two versions. The main difference between both versions is that the Enterprise version is offered under subscription and the Community version is free. (Curto Díaz & Conesa Caralt, 2010).

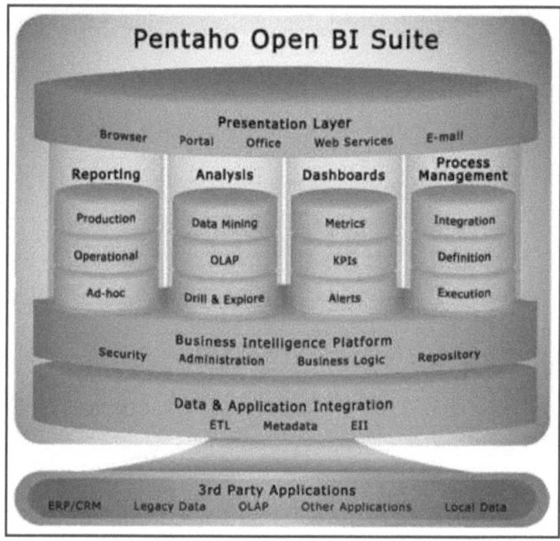

Figure 4. Pentaho Platform.
Source: (COGNUS, 2008)

2.3.5 DataWareHouse

It is a data repository that provides a global, common and integrated view of an organisation's data regardless of how it is subsequently used by consumers or users, with the following properties: stable, consistent, reliable and with historical information. Covering a global scope of the organisation and with a broad historical scope, the volume of data can be very large (hundreds of terabytes). Relational databases are the most commonly used technical support for storing these data structures and their large volumes. In short, it has the following characteristics:

- Theme-oriented: Organises a collection of information around a central theme.
- Integrated: includes data from multiple sources and presents data consistency.
- Time-varying: snapshots of the data are made based on dates or events.
- Non-volatile: read-only for end-users (Curto Díaz & Conesa Caralt, 2010).

The work of building a corporate DataWareHouse can generate inflexibilities, or be costly and require timeframes that organisations are not willing to accept. Partly for these reasons, DataMart was born. (Lluis Cano, 2007).

For the construction of a DataWareHouse, certain factors must be taken into account when evaluating a technological alternative:

- **DataWareHouse size**, the volume of data contained in the DataWareHouse.
- **Complexity of the data schema**, if the data model is complex it may hinder optimisation and query performance.

- **Number of concurrent users**, this is a determining factor if different users can launch concurrent queries (several at the same time), the DataWareHouse must manage its resources to answer the different queries.

Complexity of the queries: If the queries need to access a large number of tables and the calculations to be performed are complex, we can put the DataWareHouse database engine in difficulties. (Lluis Cano, 2007).

2.3.6 DataWareHousing

It is the process of extracting and filtering data from the common operations of the Organisation, from the different operational and/or external Information Systems, to transform, integrate and store them in a data warehouse in order to access them to support the decision making process of an Organisation. (Curto Díaz & Conesa Caralt, 2010).

2.3.7 DataMart

They are aimed at a community of users within the organisation, which may consist of the members of a department, or users at a certain organisational level, or a multidisciplinary working group with common objectives. DataMart stores information from a limited number of areas, e.g. marketing and sales or production. They are usually defined to respond to very specific uses.

DataMart are typically smaller than DataWareHouse. They have less information, fewer business models and are used by fewer users.

DataMart can be independent or dependent. The former are fed directly from information sources, while the latter are fed from the corporate DataWareHouse. Independent DataMarts can perpetuate the problem of "information silos" and in their evolution can generate inconsistencies with other DataMarts. (Lluis Cano, 2007).

DataMart is a subset of the DataWareHouse data whose objective is to respond to a specific analysis, function or need, with a specific user population. As in a DataWareHouse, the data is structured in star or snowflake patterns, and a DataMart can be dependent or independent of a DataWareHouse. For example, a possible use would be for data mining or for marketing information. The DataMart is intended to meet the needs of a workgroup or a certain department within the organisation. (Curto Díaz & Conesa Caralt, 2010).

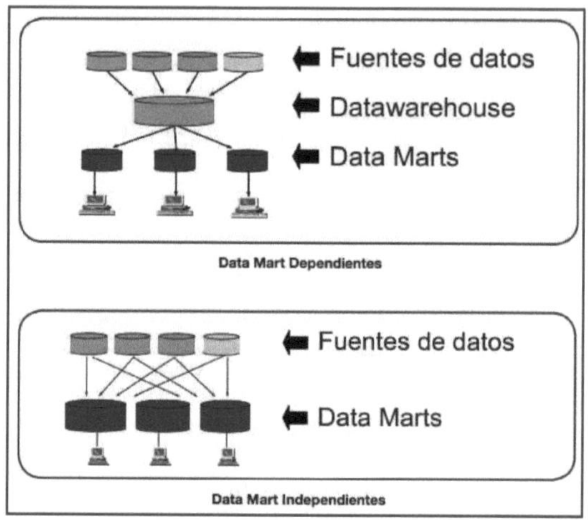

Figure 5. Types of Data Mart.
Source: (Lluis Cano, 2007).

2.3.8 Online Transactional Processing (OLTP)　Data

Among the BI methodologies, the best known and most widespread is the Kimball Methodology. Online Analytical Processing (OLAP) aims to streamline the query of large volumes of information. It uses multidimensional structures, known as OLAP cubes, which have pre-calculated and aggregated data. These systems have a much higher response speed than OLTP systems. A cube is a multidimensional vector, with N dimensions, although its name might initially lead us to believe that it only has three dimensions. In it, the information is stored in each of these dimensions, in an ordered and hierarchical way, which helps us to carry out a quick analysis of its content. A multidimensional database can contain several of these OLAP cubes. (Ramos, 2011).

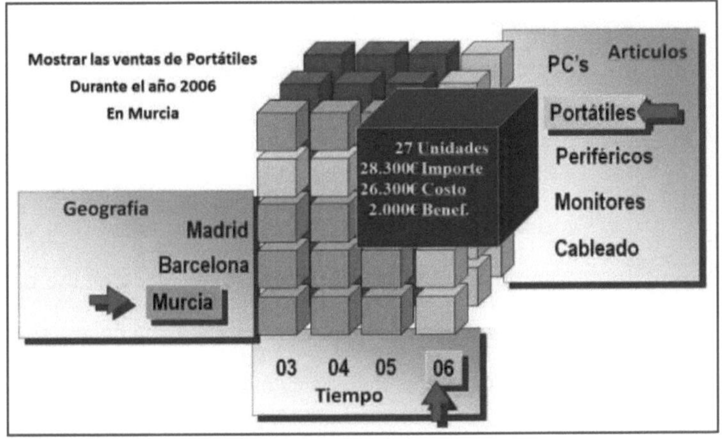

Figure 6. OLAP cubes.
Source: (Ramos, 2011)

2.3.9 Dimension

It is the representation in DataWareHouse of a view for a certain business process. If we look at the previous figure, we can observe which item I buy, in time or date or in the different geography performed. These concepts can be considered as views for this business process it can be interesting to retrieve all the purchases made by a customer. This makes us understand why we identify it as a dimension. (Curto Díaz & Conesa Caralt, 2010).

2.3.10 ETL (Extraction, Transformation and Loading) process

These are known as Extraction, Transformation and Load processes. This implies that there must be a series of processes that read the data from the different sources, transform and adapt them to the model that we have defined, clean and purify them, and introduce them into this target database. It is very important to design a good ETL process, in which all the data from the different sources must be reconciled, the necessary calculations must be made, the quality of the data must be improved, and of course, the data must be adapted to the new physical model and stored in it. (Ramos, 2011).

It is the DataWareHouse representation of a view for a certain business process. If we look at the figure above, we can observe which item I buy, in time or date or in the different geography realised.

2.3.11 Key Business Indicators (KPIs)

It is the DataWareHouse representation of a view for a certain business process. KPIs are used by organisations to assess whether they are achieving their objectives. Once they have analysed their mission, identified their stakeholders and defined their objectives, organisations need a system to measure their progress towards achieving their objectives.

KPIs are the appropriate instruments to do this   . KPIs should be quantifiable and should measure improvements in those areas where the

Activities that are critical to the success of the organisation.

KPIs should be related to the objectives and core activities of our organisation (those that enable us to deliver the results). For example, in telephone sales, it is essential to answer calls before they hang up; therefore, the percentage of calls answered before 20 seconds could be a KPI.

Different companies in the same sector may have different KPIs depending on their business models, objectives or their own idiosyncrasies.

If we establish KPIs by department, they should be aligned with each other and with the organisation's objectives.

The KPIs we choose should consider:

- Reflect business objectives.

- Be critical in order to achieve success.

- Be measurable and comparable.

- Enable corrective actions. (Lluis Cano, 2007).

2.3.12 Dashborads (Management Dashboards)

These are normally used by the Executive and Management level to monitor performance through a limited number of KPIs and compare them against corresponding targets.

These are those that provide information on the company's performance at the level of the different areas that make up the company.

This type of analysis is normally generated for directors, managers and other decision-makers within the organisation, i.e. for those who need an overall view of business performance and for whom a simple and quick presentation should be made. Some objectives that this type of business intelligence style should have:

- It should be possible to visualise key business data in a graphical format.
- Simple visual representation of KPIs.
- Performance results should be transmitted quickly.
- Scorecards should be the first level of analysis. From there you can navigate to more detail (to analytical reports).

The information that is displayed in dashboards is usually at a general level of granularity, i.e. in this type of view, access to detailed information is not provided, or is provided in a limited way.

Typical data visualisations, including speedometers and traffic lights, provide a quick overview of the current status of the defined KPIs. (García & Harmsen, 2013).

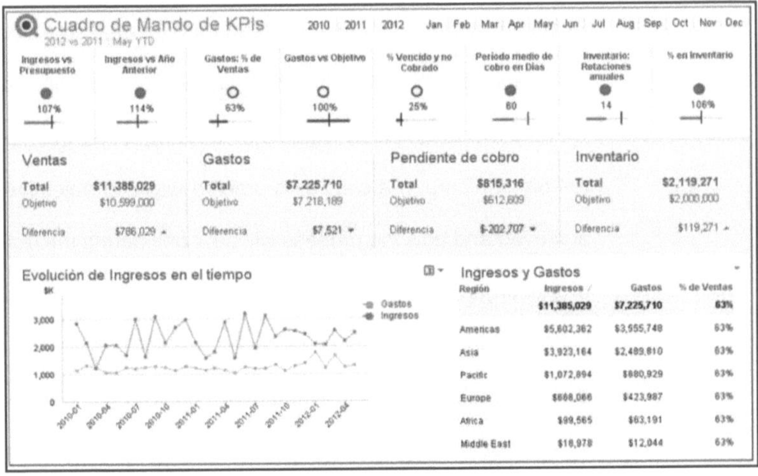

Figure 7. KPI Scorecard.
Source: (Garcia & Harmsen, 2013)

2.4   BACKGROUND TO THE RESEARCH

2.4.1   National Background

(Takimoto Aldave, 2013)in the development of his Master's thesis entitled "Methodological application of Business Intelligence in the decision-making process of EGEMSA", which had as objectives of his research, Establish a methodological application of optimization of the decision-making process based on Business Intelligence in Empresa de Generación Eléctrica Machupicchu S.A., Define a set of standards and metrics to support the decision-making process, Identify the types of information that are appropriate for the decision-making process, Evaluate methods, techniques and tools related to access, use and management of data and information. He also concludes that with the implementation of this methodology it has been possible to communicate in a clear and precise way the objectives to be achieved and how the process will be, considering the real needs of the organisation. He also concludes that we must take into account that for the success of the project it is necessary the support of the top management of the company, the formation of a multidisciplinary team formed by members of both the business areas and Information Technologies.

(Rojas Zaldivar, 2014)In the development of his thesis entitled "Implementation of a DataMart as a business intelligence solution, under the methodology of Ralph Kimball to optimise decision making in the Finance Department of the Comptroller General of the Republic", the objectives of his research were the implementation of a DataMart as a business intelligence solution, under the methodology of Ralph Kimball, to optimise decision making in the Finance Department of the Comptroller General of the Republic. Analyse the processes of the transactional base, design the multidimensional model, build the DataMart, based on the methodology of Ralph Kimball, fulfilling the requirements of the finance department and design the client interface for the deployment of the cube. The conclusions of this research were that the processes that lead to decision making were identified. The data for the development of the business intelligence solution was analysed and selected. An OLAP data model was built for the different pre-developed queries. The interfaces to deploy the OLAP cube were designed, using the Qlik View tool.

(Tume Ayala, 2014)in the development of his thesis entitled "Development of Business Intelligence to analyse Financial Companies: Cajas Municipales", with which he had as objectives of his research: Develop Business Intelligence using SQL Server Analysis Services to analyse Strategic Information of Financial Companies-Municipal Banks, Use Analysis Services Business Intelligence tools such as multidimensional analysis (OLAP) and data mining (DATA MINING) to analyse Strategic information, Model the most relevant data of the Financial Entities Municipal Banks to perform multidimensional analysis and data mining, Create a data warehouse (DataWareHouse) in SQL Server, to perform data analysis through Online Analytical Processing (OLAP), or multidimensional analysis and development of models through data mining, Design the dimensions and DataMart necessary to perform multidimensional analysis and data mining, Generate competitive advantages in financial companies - municipal savings banks through business intelligence. Likewise, the research, which has reached the following conclusions: The business intelligence tool (multidimensional analysis and data mining) was developed for the micro-financial institutions Cajas Municipales, Data mining has allowed predictions of placements in the micro-financial institutions Cajas Municipales. Thus, of the loans granted, 50.30% are used for working capital, 23.30% for consumption and 6.4% for fixed assets, among others. In addition, 96.7% of the loans granted were made with the microfinance institution's own capital, 1.6% from Agrobanco, 0.9% from Banco de la Nación and 0.8% from Cofide (both cases Cofide and Agrobanco).8% Cofide (in both cases the Naive Bayes algorithm was used). The multidimensional analysis helped to carry out a comparative analysis of the deposits and financial statements of the microfinance institutions (Caja Municipal de Ahorro y Crédito de Piura has obtained the highest net financial margin, followed by Caja Municipal de Ahorro y Crédito de Arequipa), However, in general there was a drop in the results of all the Municipal Savings and Loan Associations in 2009 compared to 2008 and 2007, probably due to the global financial crisis that occurred during that year. Thus it is obtained that most of the loans granted have been with interest rates (TEM) between 3.4% and 4.2% (the algorithm of Decision Trees was used). The information system helped the decision making of the users at the strategic and tactical levels of the different microfinance institutions - Caja Municipales. Thus, it is concluded that the Manager or Head of Savings should invest in advertising or reward policies that encourage the saving of CTS, because it is low in relation to fixed-term deposits. In addition, the Manager or Head of Savings has to implement financial management tools that allow companies to bet on the Cajas Municipales.

(Nuñez Soto, 2010)In the development of his thesis entitled "Analysis, Design and Implementation of a Business Intelligence Solution for the Finance area of the Metropolitan Municipality of Lima", the objectives of his research were: Analysis, design and implementation of a Business Intelligence Solution for this area, to meet the requirements of information related to the execution of income, expenditure and indicators that allow adequate control of municipal management, to eliminate dependence on the Systems Area to make the requirement of data, to allow users to access the required reports, to allow the municipal management data are in a single repository. Likewise, the research, in which it has reached the following conclusions: The project meets the objective of carrying out the analysis, design and implementation of the business intelligence solution,

The solution allows to eliminate the dependence on the Systems Area to make the requirement of the data. Users can access the information through the developed solution. The solution allows users to access the required reports. This eliminates the degree of error that is generated when users prepare the reports manually. The solution allows municipal management data to be found in a single repository. This allows users to access historical data.

2.4.2   International Background

(Bustos Barrera & Mosquera Artieda, 2013)In their thesis entitled "Analysis, design and implementation of a Business Intelligence solution for the generation of indicators and performance control in the company Otecel S.A., using the Hefesto 2.0 Methodology", with the following objectives: To implement a BI solution for the testing area of the Construction Management of the company Otecel S.A., by means of research, analyse the information of commercial plans activations and task registration by suppliers, delivered by the testing area of the Construction Management of the company Otecel S.A., by means of research, analyse the information of commercial plans activations and task registration by suppliers, delivered by the testing area of the Construction Management of the company Otecel S.A. To analyse the information of activations of commercial plans and registration of tasks on the part of suppliers, delivered by the area of tests of the Management of Construction, To design the structure of which they will have the dimensions and pertinent cubes, To create the design of the analysis view and the navigability that will have the pertinent information to each DataMart, Implementation of a BI solution, using Pentaho Conmunity Edition (CE) tools, Use the Report Designer tool to create and design the reports corresponding to each DataMart, Determine the data sources, with which the BI solution will work. Likewise, the research, which has reached the following conclusions: The implementation of the BI solution for the area of Tests of the Construction Management of the Company Otecel S.A., For the installation of the necessary utilities to implement the BI solution, the operation of the Pentaho Community tool was investigated, based on manuals, online searches and reading books, to adequately configure the environment in which it was required to work with the development of the application. Determining that it is an intuitive, manageable, multiplatform, simple tool when integrating data, and most importantly, as it is Open Source, the components required for the generation of additional information is accessible. The use of the Hephaestus methodology, allowed to easily identify objectives and results achieved, which are simple to understand, The use of the Hephaestus methodology made it possible to easily identify objectives and results achieved, which are simple to understand, thus determining the business needs, based on user requirements, thus involving the user at each stage for timely decision-making in the face of business changes, thanks to its adaptable structure, The use of the Hephaestus methodology made it possible to easily identify objectives and results achieved, which are simple to understand, thus determining the business needs, In order to define the necessary data source and identify its functionality, a close relationship was maintained with the user in the collection of requirements, thus understanding the business logic and defining the key indicators for analysis and decision making, We proceeded to implement the BI solution, following the phases included in the Hefesto methodology, coupling the solution to the technological infrastructure managed by Telefónica Movistar, using the production database, the internal network so that users can access the application hosted on one of its servers. The Pentaho Community tool (Data Integration), allows the updating of data in a simple way, so that at the time of obtaining the indicators, final results are obtained based on up-to-date information, maintaining the transformations and calculations made in the initial load, which will be automatically applied in subsequent updates.

(Acosta Medellin & Florez Lara, 2015)In their thesis title "Design and implementation of a BI prototype using a Big Data tool for SMEs Technology Distributor Companies", with the following objectives: Design and implement a BI prototype, using a Big data tool for a SME Technology Distributor company, Identify the current situation in terms of BI and Big data strategy in two SME Technology Distributor companies, Identify and specify BI and Big Data tools applicable to SME Technology Distributor companies, Design a BI prototype using Big Data tools for a technology distribution company, Implement BI prototype simulation using Big Data tools in a specific process of an SME technology distribution company, Validate the BI and Big Data prototype in an SME technology distribution company. Likewise, the research, which has reached the following conclusions: After the design and implementation of this prototype can be understood as companies that use information for analysis and knowledge generation take a basis of good direction to take in the market as it allows them to be able to rely on to make decisions of the same, highlighting the primordial and fundamental role that makes the Business Intelligence with supporting Big data in providing knowledge and decision making. With this model, the company would be able to know at all times the state of the sales force, analyse profitability by brands, products, etc. Depending on the need at the time, it will allow them to have the power to observe the company as a whole. The indicators that are configured as main provide alerts on the performance of each process that the company wants to apply, all this in order to lead the company to its growth and market management, In the course of the development of the thesis we seek that this prototype is a gateway to these terms for any business including large companies such as medium-sized, since it would not require a large budget for implementation, nor the sophisticated use of applications. This being one of the most interesting items that a Business Intelligence solution with the help of a Big Data tool that allows companies to have the same capabilities and performance potential as a more sophisticated software, so that as in the case of the example company can focus on other aspects such as production and sales, on the other hand, to carry out this project allows to know in more depth the concept of Big Data from the hand of Business Intelligence. Knowing its origins, what concepts are included in it, the techniques and different tools, application of all these concepts and most importantly the practice towards the challenge of work, it is achieved that the company where it was implemented had a knowledge not only of the terms used but get to think about possible changes in structure so that this valuable resource such as information is of daily support and is not seen as just storage, The success of this development is primarily in the analysis by products, brands and customers that the solution offers, reducing the reporting to a few steps and time. In addition, it provides a more dynamic way to analyse key information for the organisation and the generation of possible alerts that impact on the indicators.

(Rodriguez, 2007)In his master's thesis entitled "Methodological guide for the implementation of a business intelligence type information system that supports decision making in the academic area, at the Institución Universitaria Antonio José Camacho", the objectives are as follows: To elaborate a methodological guide for the implementation of an information system oriented to support decision making based on the results obtained in the academic area of the Institución Universitaria Antonio José Camacho, To elaborate a methodology for the implementation of business intelligence type information systems in the University institution, To formulate and answer key questions about the functioning of the institution through management indicators, To generate consolidated reports at the level of personnel with responsibilities in the strategic and tactical area of the organisation. Likewise, the research, in which it has reached the following conclusions: The business intelligence type system bases its heart on the design of a DataMart, a technology that allows tactical and strategic users to have different reports for the company, reports that can be customised for a specific purpose, as well as having the information at a minimum level of detail in the same graphic interface or system. In the project a methodological guide was proposed as a contribution and formal method in the faculty of engineering for students who want to start projects in information systems oriented to decision making, and in this way these projects are strengthened, achieving more durable information systems that are really planned based on business processes. For the automation of processes, small emerging applications were implemented in the offices of university welfare and the faculty of engineering, applications that automate processes, improve activities and serve as data sources for the business intelligence type system.

(Nadel, 2004)developed his master's thesis entitled "University Management Support System", whose research objectives were to provide the construction of a decision support application, involves the implementation of a Data Warehouse that covers all areas and departments of the University, also proposes part of the application development process in the area of Business Intelligence of the University, to fulfill this purpose of development was used the methodology Metrics version 3, integrating with the methodology of construction and operation of Data Warehouse. The project management process, with its tasks of planning, estimation, monitoring and control, together with its evaluation, allowed the work to be completed in the estimated time and with the desired quality. The COCOMO II - Composition of Applications - method of time estimation for the system development tasks has proved to be very accurate because the calculated estimate does not differ from the actual net time consumed.

2.5 Business Intelligence Solution Development Methodologies.

2.5.1 Hephaestus Methodology

Created by the engineer Ricardo Darío Bernabeu, it allows the construction of DataWareHouse in a simple, orderly and intuitive way. The construction and implementation of a DataWareHouse can be very well adapted to any software development life cycle, except that, for some phases in particular, the actions to be performed will be very different. What should be kept in mind is not to engage in methodologies that require extensive requirements gathering and analysis phases, time-consuming monolithic development phases and lengthy deployment phases. The aim is to deliver a first implementation that satisfies a part of the needs, to demonstrate the advantages of the DataWareHouse and to motivate the end-users.

It starts by collecting the information needs of the users and obtaining the key business questions. Then, the indicators resulting from the questions and their respective analysis perspectives must be identified, by means of which the conceptual data model of the DataWareHouse will be built. Then, the OLTPs will be analysed to point out the correspondences with the source data and select the fields of study for each perspective. Once this is done, the logical model of the repository will be built, making explicit the hierarchies that will be involved. Finally, the processes of loading, transformation, extraction and cleaning of the source data will be defined. (Bernabeu, 2007).

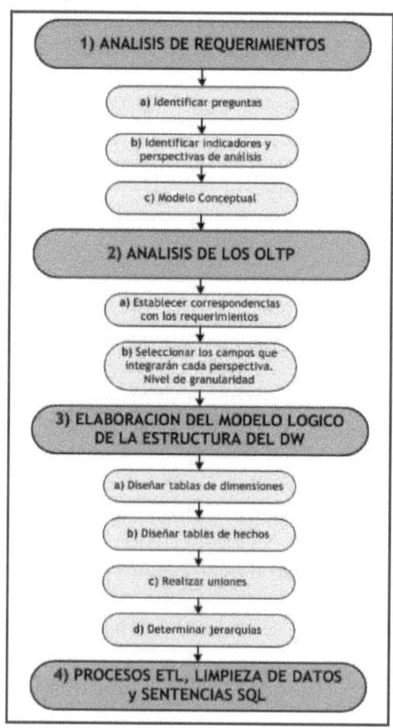

Figure 8. Hephaestus methodology.
Source: (Bernabeu, 2007).

This methodology has certain characteristics:

- The objectives and expected results in each phase are easily distinguishable and simple to understand.

- It is based on user requirements, so its structure is able to adapt easily and quickly to changes in the business.

- It reduces resistance to change by involving the end-user at every stage to make decisions regarding the behaviour and functions of the DataWareHouse.

- It uses conceptual and logical models, which are easy to interpret and analyse.

- It is independent of the type of life cycle used to contain the methodology.

- It is independent of the tools used for its implementation.

- It is independent of the physical structures containing the DataWareHouse and their respective layout.

- When a phase is completed, the results obtained become the starting point for carrying out the next step.

- Applies to both DataMart and DataWareHouse. (Bernabeu, 2007).

2.5.2 Ralph Kimball Methodology

According to the authors (Kimball & Ross, 2013)they mention that this development methodology has the following phases:

- **Project planning and management**, this first phase determines the company's readiness for a

DataWareHouse project, develops the preliminary approach, business justification and feasibility assessments.

- **Definition of Business Requirements,** For this phase it is important to bear in mind that a determining factor in the success of a Data Warehouse process is the correct interpretation of the different levels of requirements expressed by the different user groups.

- **Dimensional Modelling**, The definition of business requirements determines the data needed to meet the analytical requirements of users. Designing the data models to support these analyses requires a different approach to that used in operational systems.

- **Physical Design**, For the physical design of the database, the focus is on the selection of the structures necessary to support the logical design. A major element of this process is the definition of database environment standards.

- **Data Presentation Design and Development**, This stage is typically the most underestimated of the tasks in a DataWareHouse project. The main activities in this lifecycle phase are extraction, transformation and loading (ETL). Extraction processes are defined as those required to obtain the data to load the designed Physical Model.

- **Technical Architecture Design**, DataWareHouse environments require the integration of numerous technologies. Three factors must be taken into account: the business requirements, the current technical environments and the company's planned future technical and strategic directions in order to establish the technical architecture design of the DataWareHouse environment.

- **Product Selection and Installation**, Using the technical architecture design as a framework, it is necessary to evaluate and select the specific components of the architecture, such as the hardware platform, database engine, ETL tool, access tools, etc.

- **Specification of Applications for End-Users**, Not all DataWareHouse users need the same level of analysis. This is why at this stage the roles or user profiles for the different types of applications needed are identified based on the scope of the detected profiles (management, business analyst, vendor, etc.).

- Following the specification of end-user applications, the development of end-user applications involves the configuration of metadata and the construction of specific reports.

- **Implementation**, Implementation represents the convergence of technology, data and end-user applications accessible to the business user.

- **Maintenance and growth**, As is always stressed, the creation of a DataWareHouse is a process (with well-defined stages, with a beginning and an end, but of a spiral nature) that accompanies the evolution of the organisation throughout its history. It is necessary to continue with constant updates in order to follow the evolution of the goals to be achieved.

- **Project Management**, Project management ensures that life cycle activities are carried out in a synchronised manner.

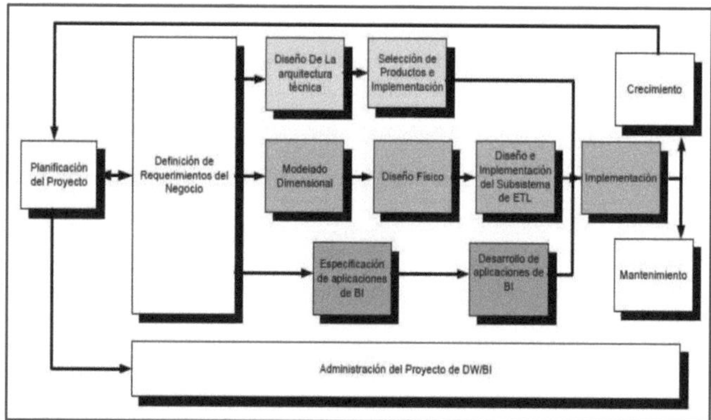

Figure 9. Stages of the Kimball Methodology.

Source: (Kimball & Ross, 2013)

Using this methodology provides benefits for the development of a Business Intelligence Solution as it starts with the development of DataMarts, to meet the specific needs of a department or area within the company, allowing better control of the information being covered, prioritising some specific business processes, and also the union of these, establish the DataWareHouse, which allows faster implementations, and lower risks, because there is less dependence between areas. This methodology is also known as **Bottom-Up**. (Sanchez Guevara, 2014)..

2.5.3 Bill Inmon Methodology

This methodology mentions that transferring the information from the different OLTP (transactional systems) of the organisations to a centralised location where the data can be used for analysis. It also insists that it must have the following characteristics:

- **Topic-oriented**: Data in the database is organised in such a way that all data elements relating to the same real-world event or object are linked together.
- **Integrated**: The database contains data from all operational systems of the organisation, and such data must be consistent.
- **Non-volatile**: Information is not modified or deleted, once a piece of data is stored, it becomes read-only information, and is retained for future reference.

- **Time-varying**: Changes in the data over time are recorded so that the reports that can be generated reflect these variations. (Sanchez Guevara, 2014)..

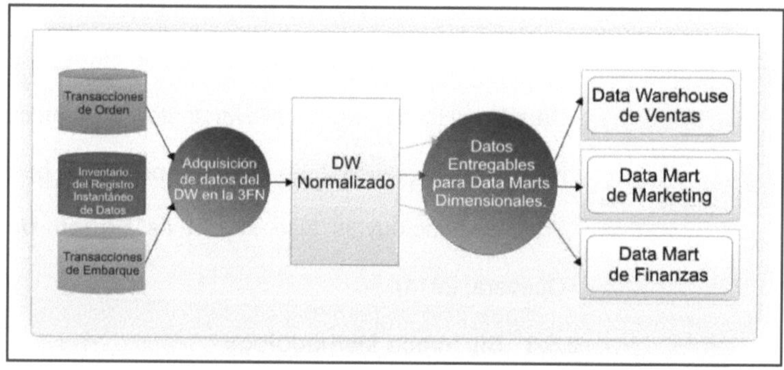

Figure 10. Bill Inmon DataWareHouse Corporate Methodology.

Source: (Sanchez Guevara, 2014)..

The information must be at the highest levels of detail. The departmental DataWareHouse or DataMarts are treated as subsets of this corporate DataWareHouse, they are built to cover the individual analysis needs of each department, and always starting from the central DataWareHouse.

The Inmon methodology is also commonly referred to as top-down. The data are extracted from the operational systems by the ETL processes and loaded into the stage area, where they are validated and consolidated in the corporate DataWareHouse, where there are also the so-called metadata that clearly and precisely document the content of the DataWareHouse. Once this process has been carried out, the refreshing processes of the departmental DataMart obtain the information from it, and with the consequent transformations, organise the data in the particular structures required by each one of them, refreshing its content. Having this global approach, it is more difficult to develop in a simple project (as we will try to address the "whole", from which we will then go to the "detail"). (Sanchez Guevara, 2014)..

2.5.4 Josep Curto's Methodology

In the book "Introduction to Business Intelligence", the authors (Curto Díaz & Conesa Caralt, 2010) mention that the phases of a Business Intelligence Project contain the following phases:

- Analysis and Requirements.
- Modelling.
- Development.
- Production.
- Training and documentation.

The focus of this methodology proposed by Curto and Conesa is the methodology already consolidated in multiple projects and on which all current developments are based.

This methodology shows one main advantage, which is that the way of developing a Business Intelligence application is quite practical, i.e. it is application-oriented and open source. (Curto Díaz & Conesa Caralt, 2010).

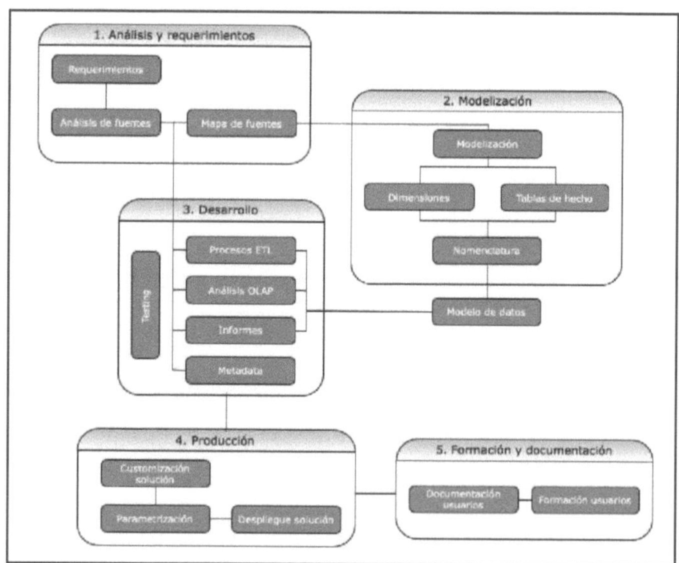

Figure 11. Phases of a BI Project.

Source: (Curto Díaz & Conesa Caralt, 2010)..

2.5. 5 Ricardo Darío Mendoza's Methodology

In his research, the engineer (Mendoza Rivera, 2010)In his research, the engineer mentions that in the BI projects developed with his ROAD MAP Methodology, which refers to Ralph Kimball and Cognos, which has the following phases:

- **Planning**, includes the Project Plan.
- **Requirement and Business Analysis**, here it contemplates the Requirement itself and the Dimensional Analysis.
- **Design**, here it contains the dimensional design and the prototype design.
- **Construction**, here contains the implementation as such: DataMart, ETL, creation of cubes, Implementation of KPIs, Data Mining, prepare Interfaces.
- **Deployment**, this is the actual implementation. (Mendoza Rivera, 2010).

In the image, it refers to the ROAD MAP methodology, for the construction of a DataWareHouse Solution.

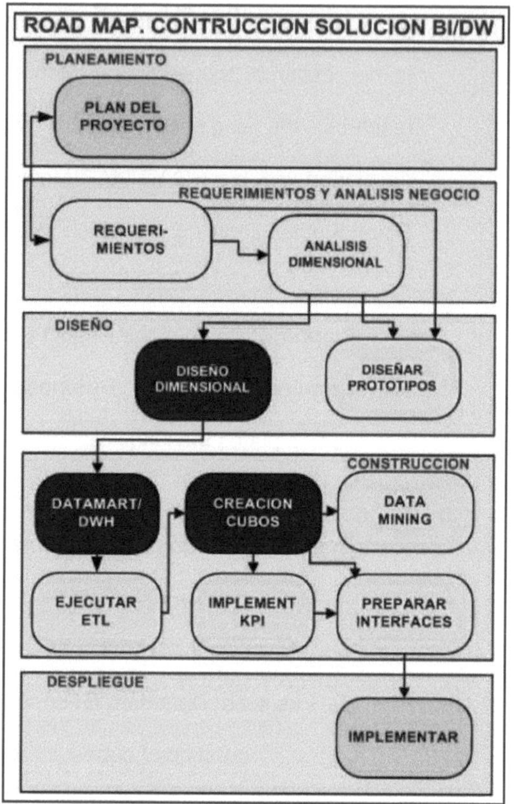

Figure 12. Phases of a BI Project.
Source: (Mendoza Rivera, 2010)

In order to start with the analysis of the information requirements, they are oriented towards the identification of dimensions and measures. Here, sources of information are available, such as: Interviews, analysis of management reports and review of the transactional database, (Mendoza Rivera, 2010).

Type Function	Source of information	Find
Management (System Content)	Interviews	Measurements and Dimensions
	Management Reporting	Measurements and Dimensions
Information Technologies	Transactional Database	Verify and validate if the dimensions and measures are in the database.

Table 01. Sources of Requirements.

Source: (Mendoza Rivera, 2010)

And based on the Dimensional technique, we will be able to identify the dimensions; therefore we proceed to apply the multidimensional technique of analytical requirements.

Dimensional Technique	Description	Example
What?	Referring to the reason for the process. What is being done.	Expenditure Accounts.
Who?	Those who demand or carry out the Que.	Supplier.

Where?	Responds to the place, where the What takes place and between Whom.	Organisation.
When?	Moment of time, where the transaction takes place.	Time.

Table 02. Multidimensional technique.

Source: (Mendoza Rivera, 2010)

Methodologically, we obtain the dimensions based on the dimensional technique, lacking the degree of granularity. This consists of identifying the minimum detail of the analysis of the information, the lowest level of detail and the capacity to analyse the detail of the data is obtained.

The grain is the specification where the measures are generated and in which the dimensions are present with an attribute that represents it. (Mendoza Rivera, 2010)

2.6   Business Intelligence Solution Development Tools.

Among the development tools, we will study those that are on the Open Source Business Intelligence (OSBI) solutions market, the most important of which is the Pentaho Suite.

2.6.1   Open Source Tools

Within the tools According to the authors (Curto Díaz & Conesa Caralt, 2010)Open Source is a software development philosophy that complies with the following principles:

- **Open**: the community has free access, use and participation of the source code, as well as the possibility of using forums to provide feedback.
- **Transparency**: the community has access to the roadmap, documentation, defects and agenda of the milestones.
- **Early & Often:** information is published frequently and early via public repositories (including source code).

In recent years, the Business Intelligence market has been enriched with Open Source solutions that cover the entire spectrum of an organisation's information exploitation needs.

2.6.2 Pentaho

According to the authors (Curto Díaz & Conesa Caralt, 2010).It is one of the most complete and mature suites in the OSBI market that has existed since 2006.

There are two versions: Community and Enterprise. It is composed of different engines included in the Pentaho server, with different tools available:

- Within **Reporting and Graphics**: Supports static, parametric and ad hoc reports, such as JFreeReport, BIRT, JaspertReport and JFreeChart.

- **OLAP Analysis and Development**: Supports OLAP (via Mondrian) and Pivot

- **Data Mining**: WEKA, YALE and other free ones such as Tiberius and WizWhy.

- **Dashboards**: Using CDF (Community Dashboard Framework), such as JBoss Portal.

- **ETL tools**: Using Kettle, Clover, Octopus and Enhydra.

- **MetaData**: which provides a business language-based information access layer.

- Database **Managers**: MySQL and PostGreSQL

- **Workflow**: the Pentaho server is based on actions that most business objects allow to launch. (Sanchez Guevara, 2014)..

Pentaho is currently following the open Core strategy, which consists of offering enhanced services and modules from an Open Source core. This is the reason why there are two versions. The main difference between the two versions is that the Enterprise version is offered on a subscription basis and the Community version is completely free.

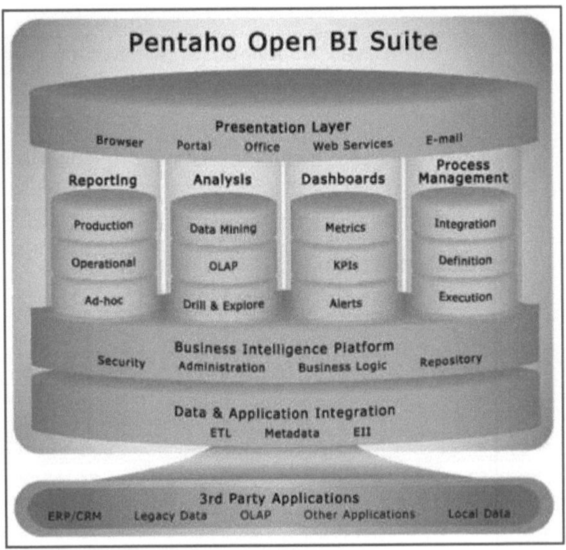

Figure 13. Pentaho Platform.
Source: (Curto Díaz & Conesa Caralt, 2010).

CHAPTER III

REQUIREMENTS, ANALYSIS AND DESIGN OF THE

SOLUTION

3.1   Analysis of information requirements

The analysis of the information requirements is oriented towards the identification of dimensions and measures. After the analysis, information sources such as interviews, analysis of management reports and review of the transactional database are used: Interviews, analysis of management reports and review of the transactional database.

In order to identify the dimensions, we applied the multidimensional analytical requirements technique.

Dimensional Technique	Description	Example
What?	Referring to the reason for the process. What is being done.	Expenditure Accounts.
Where?	Responds to the place, where the What takes place and between Whom.	Organisation.
When?	Moment of time, where the transaction takes place.	Time.
Who?	It responds to those who sued.	Supplier.

Table 03. Multidimensional technique.

Source: Own elaboration

This leads us to find the dimensions, as a product of the multidimensional technique, Dimensional Expenditure Analysis.

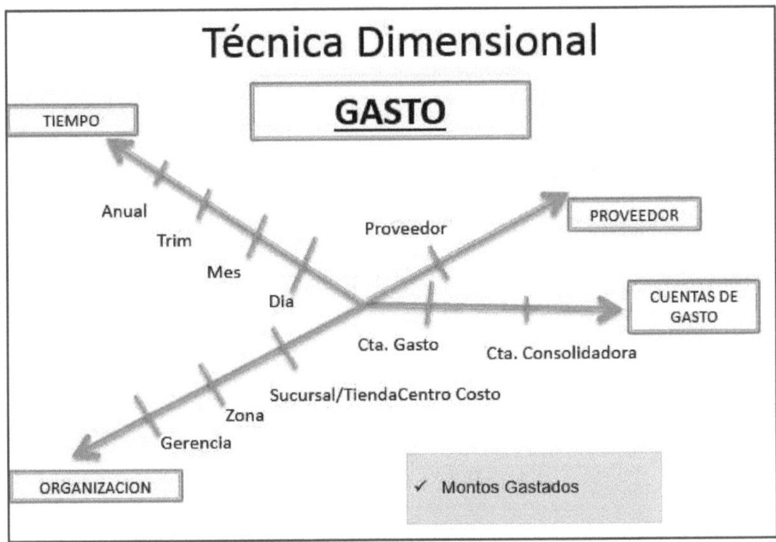

Figure 14. Dimensional Expenditure Analysis.

Source: Own elaboration

3.2 Data Identification and Exploration

The availability and analysis of the data will provide us with the opportunity cost of obtaining, identifying and exploring the information, making it convenient to review the management reports prepared by the Systems and IT area for management personnel and decision-makers.

By knowing the availability of the data, we can determine whether fundamental data integrity concepts have been applied to the ETL process.

The review of a report would involve finding measures and dimensions.

The analysis of the management report gives us more usefulness in relation to the Expenditure generated for this period (S/. 1,034 268.77), where we can see different perspectives (dimensions), in this case, for the Expenditure Account: Amounts per Cost Centre and per expenditure account, or how much was spent in this particular Time. This is where we start to make the combinations of the expenses generated in the given times by the various expense accounts, by the various cost centres.

RESUMEN GASTOS: OFICINAS ADMINISTRATIVAS			
PERIODO 2016 - PRIMER TRIMESTRE			
ENERO	**FEBRERO**	**MARZO**	**TOTAL**
MANT. LOCAL			
OFICINA MATRIZ — 1.946,50	1.310,00	9.895,00	5.850,15
AGENCIA CHICLAYO — 3.146,50	2.510,00	11.095,00	16.751,50
TOTAL MANT LOCAL — **5.093,00**	**3.820,00**	**20.990,00**	**22.601,65**
MANT. MOVIL			
OFICINA MATRIZ — 12.250,25	10.550,89	12.585,10	35.386,24
AGENCIA CHICLAYO — 13.450,25	11.750,89	13.785,10	38.986,24
TOTAL MANT. MOVIL — **25.700,50**	**22.301,78**	**26.370,20**	**74.372,48**
EMP. RECAUDOS			
OFICINA MATRIZ — 77.250,50	18.521,00	12.550,00	108.321,50
AGENCIA CHICLAYO — 78.450,50	19.721,00	13.750,00	111.921,50
TOTAL EMP. RECAUDOS — **155.701,00**	**38.242,00**	**26.300,00**	**220.243,00**
RECUPERADORES			
OFICINA MATRIZ — 4.558,25	6.500,00	9.895,00	20.953,25
AGENCIA CHICLAYO — 5.758,25	7.700,00	11.095,00	24.553,25
TOTAL RECUPERADORES — **10.316,50**	**14.200,00**	**20.990,00**	**45.506,50**
CONSULTORIAS			
OFICINA MATRIZ — 75.500,00	85.500,00	120.125,25	281.125,25
AGENCIA CHICLAYO — 76.700,00	86.700,00	121.325,25	284.725,25
TOTAL CONSULTORIAS — **152.200,00**	**172.200,00**	**241.450,50**	**565.850,50**
HONORARIOS PROFESIONALES			
OFICINA MATRIZ — 25.652,12	15.500,20	9.895,00	51.047,32
AGENCIA CHICLAYO — 26.852,12	16.700,20	11.095,00	54.647,32
TOTAL HONORARIOS — **52.504,24**	**32.200,40**	**20.990,00**	**105.694,64**
*****TOTALES********* — **401.515,24**	**282.964,18**	**357.090,70**	**1.034.268,77**

Figure 15. Management Report - Sample.
Source: Own elaboration

3.3 Data Extraction, Data Transformation and Data Loading

Financial institutions forecast a lot of their costs, but especially the margin of the expenses generated in the year. For the present study, we will identify, based on the dimensional technique, the dimensions and the degree of granularity. This consists of identifying the minimum detail of the analysis of the information, according to the analysis carried out previously. We will obtain, we will reach the lowest level of detail and the ability to analyse the detail of the data.

Dimensions and levels, after the review of the dimensional technique, we obtain the dimensions and levels for our study.

Dimensions	Levels
Cost Centre	Cost Centre, Management, Zone.
Expenditure Account	Account, grouping account.
Weather	Date, year, month, day, semester, quarter, weekday.
Supplier	Supplier.

Table 4. Dimensions and levels.
Source: Own elaboration

We will now look at dimensions and hierarchies.

DIMENSIONS	HIERARCHIES					
	LEVEL 1	LEVEL 2	LEVEL 3	LEVEL 4	LEVEL 5	LEVEL 6
Cost Centre	Cost Centre	Management	Zone			
Expenditure Account	Expenditure Account	Grouping account				
Weather	Date	Year	Month	Day	Semester	Quarter
Supplier	Supplier					

Table 5. Dimensions and Hierarchies.
Source: Own elaboration

We will now look at the dimensions and measurements.

MEASUREMENTS	DIMENSIONS			Supplier
	Cost Centre	Expenditure Account	Weather	Supplier
Amount Spent Soles	x	x	x	x
Amount Spent Dollars	x	x	x	x

Table 6. Dimensions and measurements.
Source: Own elaboration

3.4 DataWareHouse design

3.4.1 Cost Centre Dimension

It contains information on the cost centres of the
financial institution, such as the management,
the area and the cost centre itself.

Field *	Type *	Collation	Null *	Key *
PkCentroCosto	int(11)	{null}	NO	PRI
CentroCosto	varchar(50)	utf8_general_ci	YES	
Gerencia	varchar(50)	utf8_general_ci	YES	
Zona	varchar(50)	utf8_general_ci	YES	
CostCenter	varchar(10)	utf8_general_ci	YES	
FECHAeXTR...	datetime	{null}	YES	

Figure 16. Cost Centre Dimension.
Source: Own elaboration

Level	Description	Example
Cost Centre	This is the description of the Cost Centres.	Training, Accounting, Tarapoto Store, Tumbes Office.

Management	It is the description of the organisation, such as the concentrating management.	Business Management, Finance Management.
Zone	Indicates the grouping of cost centres, zoned.	South Zone, North Zone, Central Zone.

Table 7. Description of the Cost Centre Dimension.
Source: Own elaboration

3.4.2 Dimension Expenditure Account

Contains information on all expense accounts, which are analysed by the Financial Institution, such as expense item accounts.

Field *	Type *	Collation	Null *	Key *
pk_cuentaGasto	int(11)	{null}	NO	PRI
CUENTA	varchar(20)	utf8_general_ci	YES	
Name_CUENTA_GASTO	varchar(30)	utf8_general_ci	YES	
CUENTA_GASTO_GRUPO	varchar(20)	utf8_general_ci	YES	
FECHAeXTRACION	datetime	{null}	YES	
id	varchar(20)	utf8_general_ci	YES	

Figure 17. Expenditure Account Dimension.
Source: Own elaboration

Level	Description	Example
Expenditure Account.	This is the description of the Expenditure	Training, rent, energy, water, fuel, notary fees, per

	Accounts used for the case study.	diems, collection companies, etc.
Group expenditure account.	It is the one that groups the expenses, or also the mother account.	Suppliers, taxes, etc.

Table 8. Description of the Expenditure Account
Dimension.
Source: Own elaboration

3.4.3 Supplier dimension

Contains information on all suppliers, which provide services to the Financial Institution.

Field *	Type *	Collation	Null *	Key *
ProveedorKey	int(11)	{null}	NO	
persona	int(11)	{null}	NO	
NomProveedor	varchar(80)	utf8_general_ci	YES	
DocumentoFiscal	int(11)	{null}	YES	
Direccion	varchar(80)	utf8_general_ci	YES	
FECHAeXTRA...	datetime	{null}	NO	

Figure 18. Supplier dimension.
Source: Own elaboration

Level	Description	Example
NomProvider.	This is the description or name of the supplier, which provides services or sells products to the Institution.	COMPUCENTER S.R.L, UNIVERSIDAD DE PIURA, MAFEC E.I.R.L., MAQUINARIAS JAAMSA, etc.

Table 9. Description of the Supplier Dimension.
Source: Own elaboration

3.4.4 Time Dimension

Contains time analysis information (year, month, week, quarter), based on the time periods, where the expenditures were incurred.

Field *	Type *	Collation	Null *	Key *
pk_tiempo	int(11)	{null}	NO	PRI
Anual	int(11)	{null}	YES	
Semestre	varchar(2)	utf8_general_ci	YES	
Trimestre	int(11)	{null}	YES	
Mes	varchar(30)	utf8_general_ci	YES	
DiaSemana	varchar(30)	utf8_general_ci	YES	
variabledate	datetime	{null}	YES	
id	varchar(10)	utf8_general_ci	YES	
FECHAeX...	datetime	{null}	YES	

Figure 19. Time dimension.
Source: Own elaboration

Level	Description	Example
Annual.	This is the year in which the expenditure is incurred.	2014,2016,2017.
Semester.	This is the six-month period in which the expenditure is incurred.	S1, S2, S3.
Trimester.	This is the quarter in which the expenditure is incurred.	1,2,3.
Month.	This is the month in which the expenditure is incurred.	April, January, December, etc.
Day week.	This is the day of the week on which the expenditure is made.	Monday, Thursday, Friday, etc.
Date.	This is the date on which the expenditure is incurred.	15/03/2016.

Table 10. Description of the Time Dimension.
Source: Own elaboration

3.4.6 Table of Facts

It contains the information of the analysis of the expenditure generated in the Financial

Institution, with the relations of its 4 dimensions and its measures.

Field *	Type *	Collation	Null *	Key *
CuentaGastoKey	int(11)	{null}	NO	PRI
TiempoKey	int(11)	{null}	NO	PRI
CentroCostoKey	int(11)	{null}	NO	PRI
ProveedorKey	int(11)	{null}	NO	PRI
MONTO_SOLES	decimal(18,2)	{null}	YES	
MONTO_DOLA...	decimal(18,2)	{null}	YES	

Figure 20. Facts and Figures - Expenditure Table.
Source: Own elaboration

Level	Description
Amount in Soles	Total amount of expenditure, generated in Soles.
Amount in Dollars	Total amount of expenditure, generated in Dollars.

Table 11. Metrics.
Source: Own elaboration

3.4.7 Final Dimensional Design

Here, as the final product of the Dimensional
Design, we obtain the dimensions, levels and
hierarchies for the DataWareHouse.

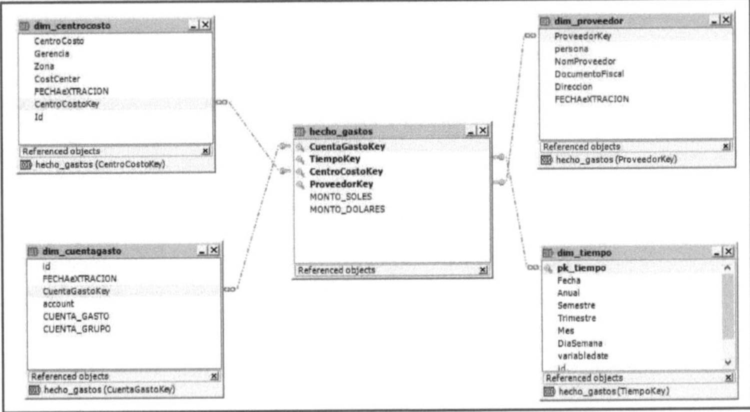

Figure 21. Final design of the DataWareHouse.
Source: Own elaboration

CHAPTER IV

IMPLEMENTATION OF THE SOLUTION

4.1 Design of the Architecture

The architecture to be followed in the solution of the present project is the ROLAP architecture, which supports aggregation, calculations and categorisation of data from standard relational databases, such as Oracle, MySQL, Microsoft SQL Server, and others.

The architecture of the solution for this project is composed of the internal data source for the DataMart, which in this case will be the transactional database of the organisation. For the ETL processes, all the operations and transformations that the data need to be stored in the DataMart will be carried out, and it will also allow the data to be integrated in the same repository (DataMart). Users will have access to the OLAP cubes for the analysis of the information by means of exploitation tools. The following figure shows the components involved in the design of the architecture of the solution.

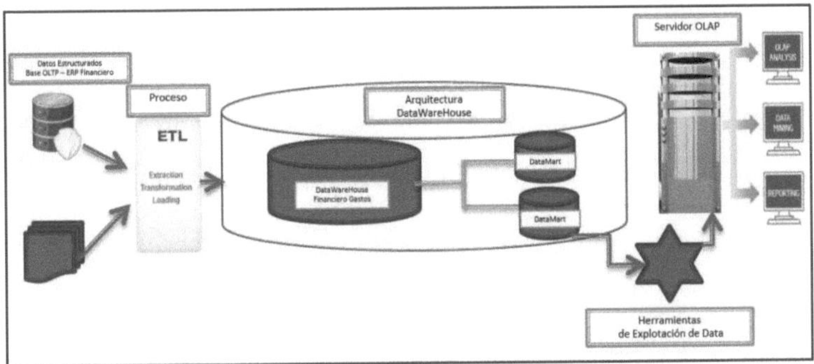

Figure 22. Business Intelligence Solution Architecture.

Source: Own elaboration

Components, Pentaho Data Integration has been used for the extraction, using Spoon as graphical interface, which performs the Extraction, Transformation and Loading under the Kitchen tool, which allows to execute Jobs, planned in Batch mode, to be executed automatically in periods of time.

MySQL WorkBench 6.3 CE was used as the database modeller for the DataWareHouse, which was used to develop the ExpenseBox and thus complement the Open Source Business Intelligence (OSBI) solution together with Pentaho BI-Server.

The OLAP tool that will be used for DataMart processing is Schema Workbench, which will be used to build the OLAP cube. Workbench is part of the Pentaho suite, its purpose is to build the OLAP cubes and manage the ROLAP query language called MDX (Multi-Dimensional Expression). The application generates and allows to modify XML files (which contain the cube schema) being able to add, delete or edit dimensions and metrics. For our analysis we will use Saiku Analytics, which is a plug-in that interacts with Pentaho Server, in itself is an OLAP tool intended for Pentaho end users; its specific function is to manipulate the cube, analysing the facts (Expenditures), from different perspectives (dimensions), it allows us to visualise and perform data analysis in an easy and intuitive way. It is an improvement of the graphical interface of the web portal, which will replace Jpivot, through which you can build your own views by dragging and dropping fields.

We will now proceed to detail the tools to be used in the BI solution architecture of this project:

a) **Internal OLTP data source**, the internal data source will be the transactional database of the Financial Entity's ERP Administrative ERP, which is implemented in SQL Server 2008/R2 Manager.

b) **ETL process**, the process (Extraction, Transformation and Loading), of the CashExpense DataMart, will allow the loading of the Data to the Dimensional Database.

c) **Expense DataMart**, This expense DataMart is a database that contains the tuples or tables that make up the structures of the designed dimensional model. This database is loaded through the execution of ETL processes.

d) **OLAP Cubes**, this component will allow the processing of large volumes of information, it will allow us to analyse the information, to exploit the data, thus being able to contribute to intelligent decision making.

e) **OLAP server**, this component allows to process MDX queries, returning multidimensional answers.

f) **Data Exploitation Tools**, the exploitation process allows us to generate dynamic reports, analysis tables, dashboards; in this way we can exploit the information we have processed.

g) **Users**, users will be able to access the Web Application, which is hosted on the Web Server, online. In this way, users will be able to generate and access reports. They can also perform data mining and modify the structure of these reports.

4.2 DataMart

As previously indicated, the tool selected for the construction of the DataMart is MySQL Workbench 5.2, which is the same one used for the physical dimensional design carried out in the dimensional design stage, that is to say, for the modelling of the database. We proceeded to create the following DataMart named **"erpcajadwh"**, the following figure shows the DataMart already implemented with its respective dimensions and the table made, awaiting the ETL process to be populated.

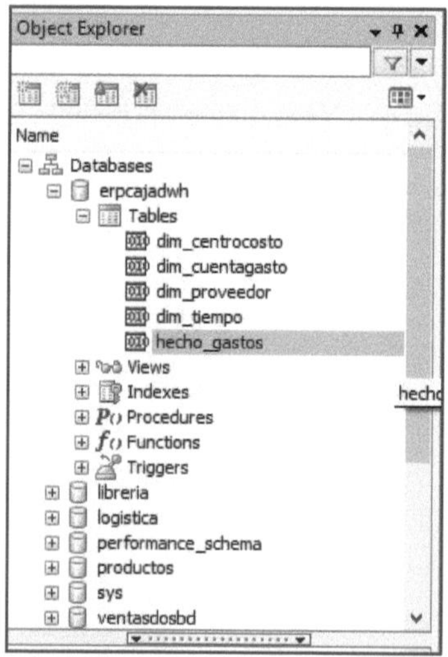

Figure 23. DataMart of the BI Solution - erpcajadwh.
Source: Own elaboration

4.3 ETL implementation

For the execution of the ETL we used the Pentaho Data Integration tool (ver.8.2), which is included in the version of

Pentaho that is being used: As a populating or loading strategy, it consists of the implementation of a task that creates a sequence of activities that provides an order of execution, they are used for a flow control, in which we generate the necessary transformations for the populating of the DataMart, within the transformations the steps or "steps" are generated (each one is designed for a specific function, to after the execution, continue with the next step, the cleaning of the dimension tables and the corresponding Facts table through a scripting which allows to execute a SQL statement, then through the transformations the population of the dimensions is performed. The transactional database is in a different database manager (MS. SQL SERVER 2008 and MySQL), showing the final population scheme under the Data Integration tool of Pentaho.

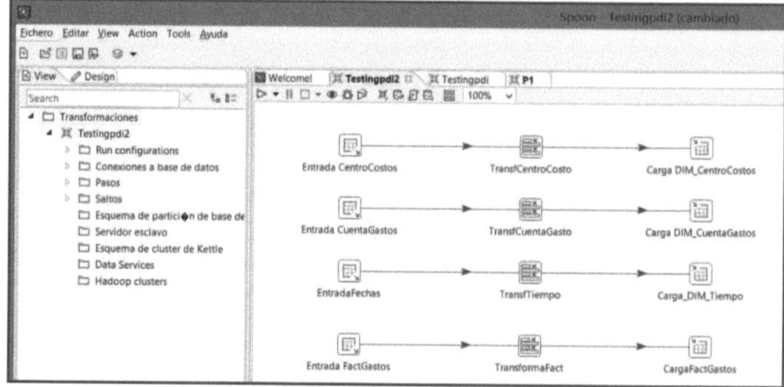

Figure 24. Populating the DataMart.
Source: Own elaboration

The loading and populating of the Fact Table, also known as Fact, in this case is the FactExpenses (Output Fact Table), the steps and their execution metrics are shown in the following image.

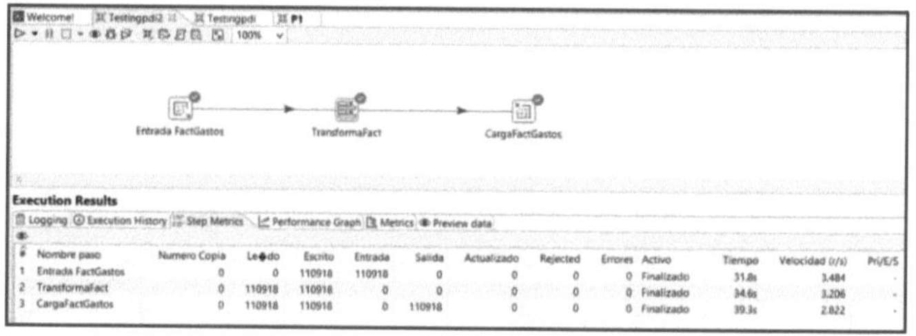

Figure 25. Loading the Fact-Fact table.
Source: Own elaboration

4.3 Creating and Loading the OLAP Cube

The OLAP cubes are developed using the Pentaho Schema Workbench tool (ver3.6.1). At the end, the final schema of the cube is obtained, the name of the schema is "ExpensesCash", which will analyse the information of the Financial Entity, with the final result shown in the following figure.

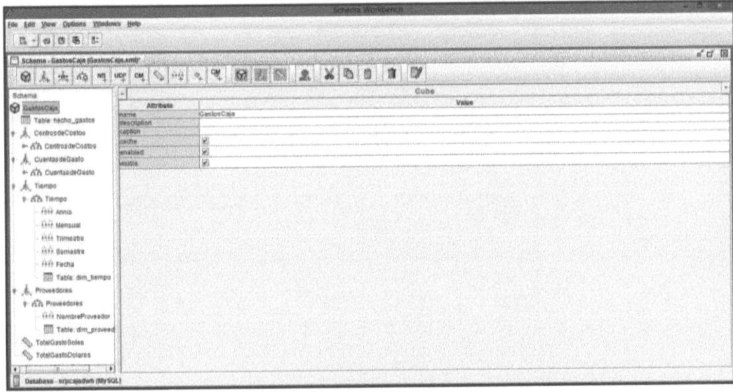

Figure 26. OLAP Cube of the BI Solution.
Source: Own elaboration

After the creation of the OLAP Cube, it is also necessary to be able to publish it, in order to be used by the Pentaho Analysis tool.

If the cube creation is successful, a message should be displayed indicating that the publication is successful, concluding the cube publication process in Schema Workbench, ready to be used with a Pentaho Analysis tool.

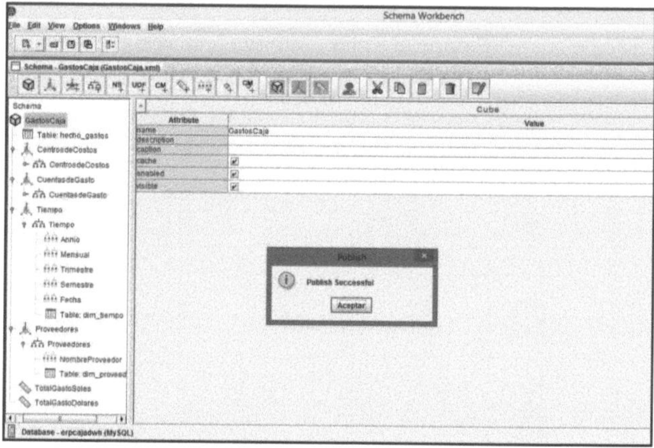

Figure 27. Publication of the OLAP Cube.
Source: Own elaboration

CHAPTER V
PRESENTATION OF RESULTS

(MULTIDIMENSIONAL ANALYSIS)

5.1 Presentation of the BI Solution

With the architecture already in place and implemented, we proceed to show the results of the graphical interface of the Pentaho BI-Server tool, which is an Open Source Business Intelligence (OSBI) solution. To do this, we start with the plug-ins that interact with Pentaho BI-Server, such as Saiku Analytics, whose specific function is to operate and manipulate the information of the Cube.

Interacting with the Cube is done from different perspectives (Dimensions), analysing the data and its facts (Cash Expenses), applying filters to the respective data, and others. Saiku Analytics, as a tool, has a wide range of graphs to analyse the facts and above all the business data.

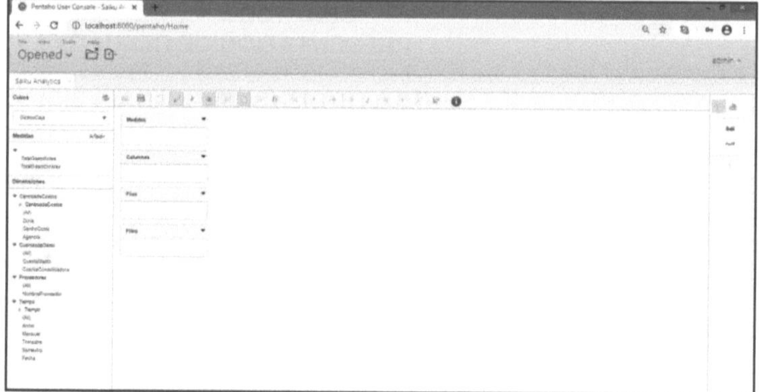

Figure 28. OLAP Cube ExpenseCase - Saiku Analytics.
Source: Own elaboration

With the Saiku Analytics interface, we can have different reports, for management analysis, counting on the availability of the Data. Here for the sample of the following image, we can observe the relation to the Expense generated for a period, where we can see different perspectives (dimensions). Here is where we start to make the combinations of the expense accounts (Dimension 01) generated in certain times (Dimension 02) by the different expense accounts, by the different cost centres (Dimension 03), by the different suppliers of services and/or products (Dimension 04).

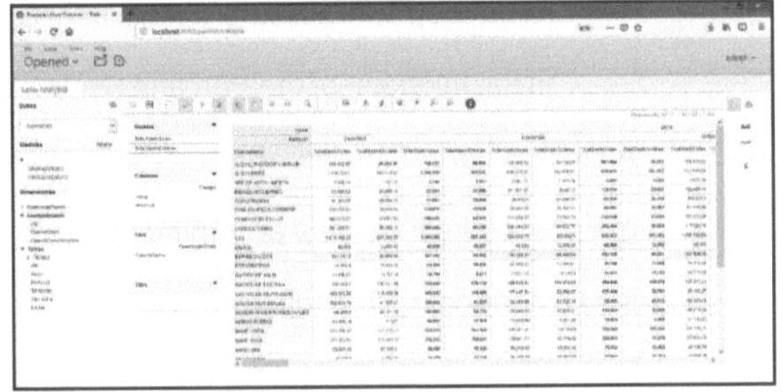

Figure 29. Expenditure Report 01.
Source: Own elaboration

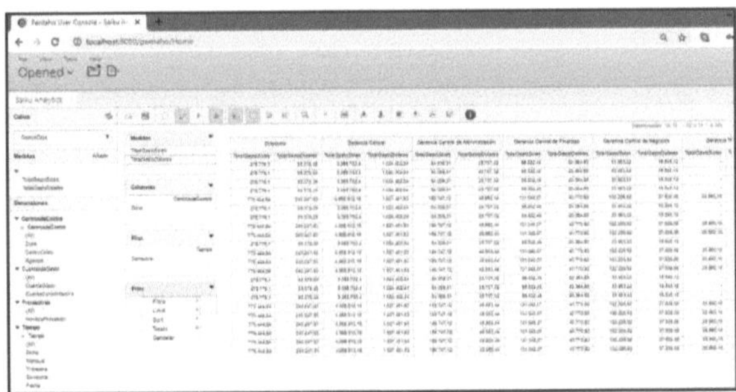

Figure 30. Expenditure Report 02.
Source: Own elaboration

5.2 Reporting and results of indicators

In the interface of the Pentaho BI-Server tool, such as Saiku Analytics, we will analyse the first PGEPPR indicator: Percentage of Expenditure Executed according to item by time period. For this solution, certain expenditure accounts were filtered, which were incurred in various monthly and annual time periods, as the following graphs show. This process can be done with various filters, depending on the analysis of expenditure in any given time period.

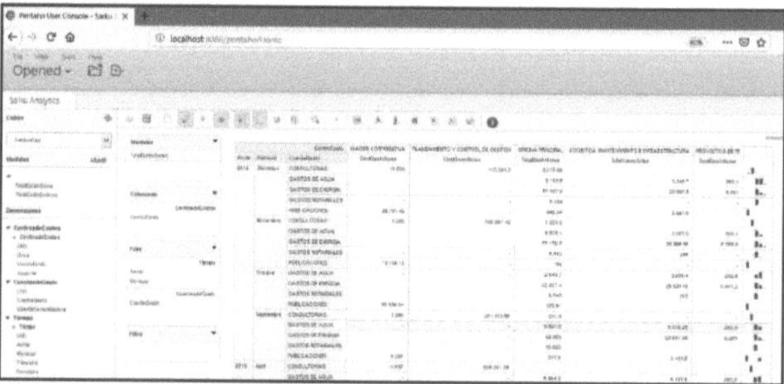

Figure 31. Expenditure incurred in Annual period.
Source: Own elaboration

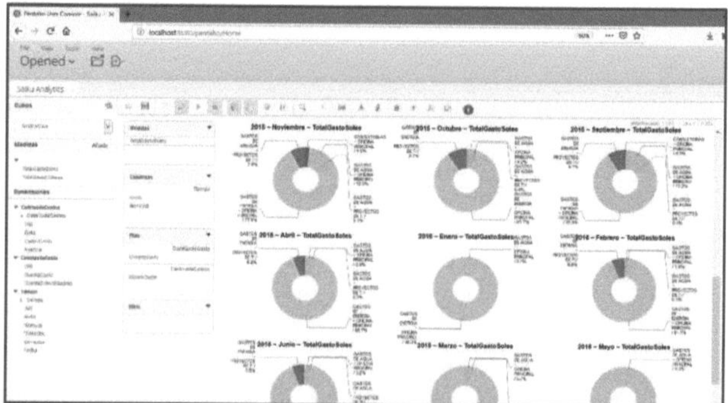

Figure 32. Percentage of Expenditure in Annual Period.
Source: Own elaboration

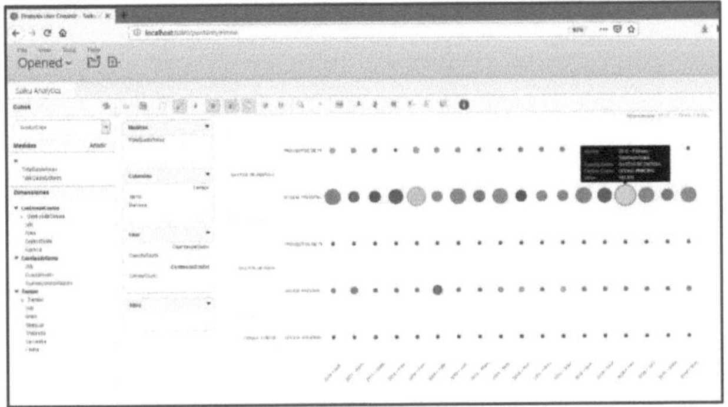

Figure 33. Percentage of Expenditure in Annual Period.
Source: Own elaboration

As a second indicator, we have the CPGR: Average by Expenditure Realised. In this solution we filtered by certain expenditure accounts, over an annual period. This process can be done with various filters, depending on the analysis of expenditure over any period of time.

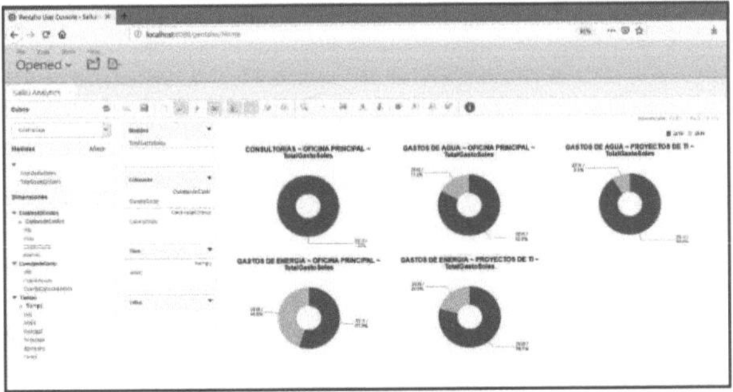

Figure 34. Average expenditure in a period.
Source: Own elaboration

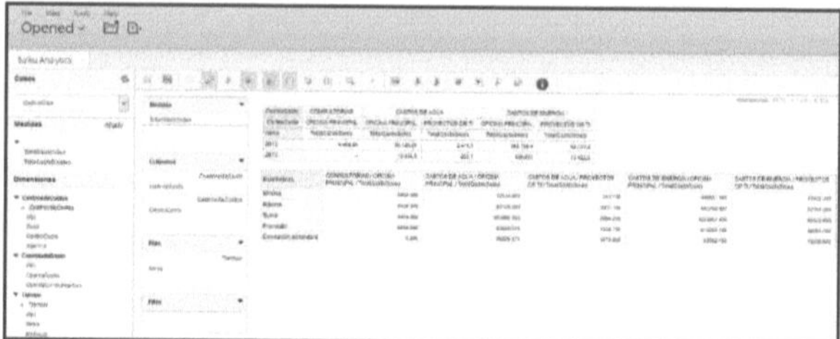

Figure 35. Average expenditure in a period.
Source: Own elaboration

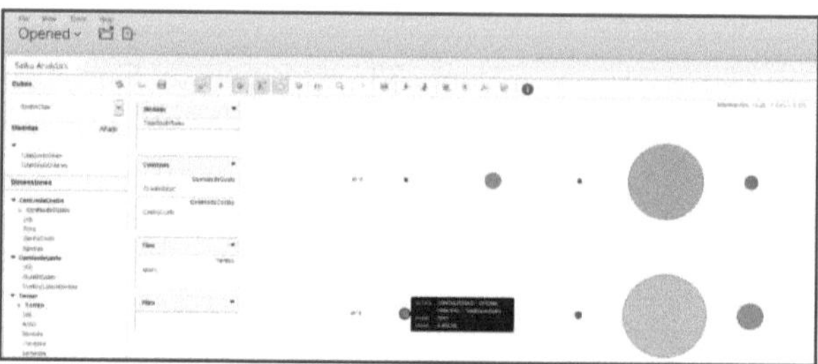

Figure 36. Average expenditure in a period.
Source: Own elaboration

As the third and last indicator, we have the TPGR: Average Time to Generate an Expense Report. For this validation we used a table similar to Table N. 10, where the values for the Pre-Test and Post-Test data are shown.

With the results obtained in the comparative table above, it can be shown that the time difference of 00:50:20 (50 minutes and 20 seconds) is the time being saved in consulting the total spent in a period of time. With this we can affirm that the Business Intelligence Solution implemented has been positive, in this indicator.

Item	Indicator	Abbreviation	Averages	
			PRE-TEST	POST-TEST
	The average time it takes to generate an expense report.	TPR	01:00:00	00:10:40

Table 12. Outcome indicator.
Source: Own elaboration

5.3 Evaluation of the Hypothesis

5.3.1 Testing the Hypothesis

Ho: The development of a business intelligence solution will not contribute to the analysis of expenditure management in a financial institution.

Ha: The development of a business intelligence solution will contribute to the analysis of expenditure management in a financial institution.

5.4 Discussion and Analysis of Results

This research work consists of validating the use of business intelligence, which will contribute to the analysis of expenditure management in a financial institution.

For this purpose, the free software platform Pentaho BI-Server has been used, being an Open Source Business Intelligence (OSBI) solution, in which it has been used for the quality and filtering of the Data, as well as the feeding or loading to the dimensional base, using for this the ETL process, with the graphic interface tool Spoon, which performs the Extraction, Transformation and Loading.

In the elaboration of the analytical cube we used the Schema Workbench (SW) tool, leaving the dimensional information ready to be used with an Analysis tool.

To interact with the Cube information, from the different perspectives or dimensions, Saiku Analytics was used, whose specific function is to operate and manipulate the Cube information.

To conclude, the models of the BI tools are implemented, by means of the indicators set out in the hypothesis, determining the confirmation of the alternative hypothesis (Ha), i.e.: *"The development of a business intelligence solution will contribute to the analysis of expenditure management in a financial institution"*, therefore, the hypothesis of the proposed research is accepted.

By contrasting the research solution, it provides further analysis details for the organisation in terms of cost analysis, which can be used for further analysis of the business in the financial area.

As a contribution of the research, it can be used in other organisations, based on the same tools and working methodologies.

Conclusions

- ✓ With the indicators set out in the hypothesis, we were able to generate a dimensional analysis model, which allowed us to validate the improvement in the analysis of expenditure in a Financial Institution, thus enabling the implementation of the Business Intelligence Solution.

- ✓ We were able to design the dimensions of the BI Solution, based on the dimensional technique, obtaining the dimensions and their degree of granularity for the analysis of the information.

- ✓ The Pentaho Data Integration (pdi) suite was used as a technological tool in the process of transforming, cleaning and loading the information, adjusting it to the business requirements.

- ✓ It was used for the design of the dimensions; building and generating the analytical cube DataWareHouse with the Schema Workbench (SW) tool, and for the multidimensional analysis the Saiku Analytics graphical interface was used.

- ✓ For the deployment of the Business Intelligence Solution, the open source software platform, the Open Source Business Intelligence (OSBI) solution was used, as well as its various tools and artefacts generated, allowing an intuitive and simple handling

for end users to generate their reports and analysis

according to their various needs.

Recommendations

✓ It is recommended for future work to use other new trends and technologies, which are emerging more strongly in the trends and tools of the fascinating world of Business Intelligence, such as Mobile BI, as well as Big Data technology in the field of microfinance, especially as it complements BI technology very well.

✓ In the present research only the open source BI platform was considered for the deployment of the model, however, the model could be extended to evaluate any type of BI platform, therefore, it is recommended for future work to apply it to other types of BI platforms that are not necessarily open source.

VI. BILIOGRAPHY

Acosta Medellin, J. N., & Florez Lara, D. H. (2015). *Design and Implementation of a BI prototype, using a Big Data tool for SMEs technology distributors.* Bogota, Colombia: Catholic University of Colombia.

(n.d.). *Analysis, Design and Implementation of a Business Intelligence Solution for the Finance Area of the Metropolitan Municipality of Lima.*

Bernabeu, R. D. (2007). *Research and Systematisation of Concepts - HEFESTO: Own Methodology for the Construction of a DataWarehouse.* Cordoba, Argentina .

Briones, G. (2002). *Methodology of quantitative research in social science.* Bogota, Colombia: ARFO Editores e Impresores Ltda.

Bustos Barrera, S. A., & Mosquera Artieda, V. N. (2013). *Analysis, Design and Implementation of a Business Intelligence solution for the generation of indicators and performance control, in the Company Otecel S.A., using the Hefesto 2.0 Methodology.* Sangolqui, Ecuador: Escuela Politecnica del Ejercito.

COGNUS. (03 September 2008). *COGNUS.* Retrieved on 07/20/2017, from Pentaho Open BI: http://www.cognus.biz/pentaho-open-bi/

Curto Díaz, J., & Conesa Caralt, J. (2010). *Introduction to Business Intelligence.* Barcelona: Editorial UOC.

García, M. Á., & Harmsen, B. (2013). *QlikView 11 for Developers.* Birmingham: Packt Publishing Ltd.

Hernández Sampieri, Roberto; Fernández Collado, Carlos; Baptista Lucio, Pilar;. (1997). *Research Methodology.* Mexico: McGraw- Hill Interamericana de México,S.A. de C.V.

intryo. (n.d.). *intryo.* Retrieved on 07/20/2017, from intryo: http://www.intryo.com/pentaho

Kimball , R., & Ross, M. (2013). *The Data Warehouse Toolkit: The Definitive Guide to Dimensional Modeling, Third Edition.* Indianapolis, EEUU.: John Wiley & Sons, Inc.

kimball, R., & Caserta, J. (2004). *The Data Warehouse ETL toolkit.* Canada: Wiley Publishing, Inc.

Lluis Cano, J. (2007). *Business Intelligence: Competing with Information.* Madrid: Banesto Fundación Cultural-ESADE.

Mendoza Rivera, R. D. (2010). *Construction of a DataWareHouse to support the improvement of decision making in the Academic and Collection Process of a Private University.* Trujillo: Universidad Cesar Vallejo.

Nadel, J. (2004). *University Management Support System.* Argentina: Instituto Tecnologico de Buenos Aires.

Nuñez Soto, G. I. (2010). *Análisis, Diseño e Implementación de una Solución de Inteligencia de Negocios para el área de Finanzas de la Municipalidad Metropolitana de Lima.* Lima: Pontificia Universidad Católica del Perú.

PENTAHO. (n.d.). *Pentaho.* Retrieved on 07/20/2017, from Mondrian: http://community.pentaho.com/projects/mondrian/

Ramos, S. (2011). *Microsoft Business Intelligence: see the bucket half full.* Spain: SolidQ Press.

Rodriguez, C. A. (2007). *Methodological guide for the implementation of a business intelligence type information system that supports decision making in the academic area at the Institución Universitaria Antonio José Camacho.* Cali: Fundación Universitaria Iberoamericana.

Rojas Zaldivar, A. (2014). *Implementation of a datamart as a business intelligence solution, under the methodology of Ralph Kimball to optimize decision making in the Finance Department of the Comptroller General of the Republic.* Chiclayo: University of San Martin de Porres.

Sanchez Guevara, O. A. (2014). *Modelo de Inteligencia de Negocios para la Toma de Decisiones en la Empresa San Roque S.A.* Trujillo: Universidad Privada Antenor Orrego.

Takimoto Aldave, J. (2013). *Aplicación Metodologica de Inteligencia de Negocios en el Proceso de Toma de Desiciones de EGEMSA.* Piura: PIRHUA Institutional Repository.

Tume Ayala, V. R. (2014). *Desarrollo de Inteligencia de Negocios para analizar Empresas Financieras: Cajas Municipales.* Piura: Universidad Nacional de Piura.

VII. TIMETABLE OF ACTIVITIES

The start date of this research project is 01.08.2017.

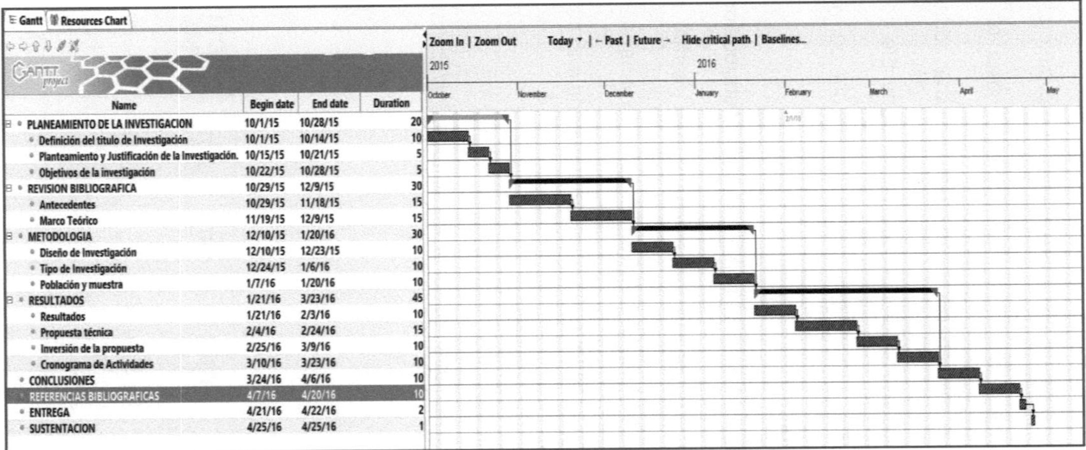

Name	Begin date	End date	Duration
PLANEAMIENTO DE LA INVESTIGACION	10/1/15	10/28/15	20
Definición del título de Investigación	10/1/15	10/14/15	10
Planteamiento y Justificación de la Investigación.	10/15/15	10/21/15	5
Objetivos de la investigación	10/22/15	10/28/15	5
REVISION BIBLIOGRAFICA	10/29/15	12/9/15	30
Antecedentes	10/29/15	11/18/15	15
Marco Teórico	11/19/15	12/9/15	15
METODOLOGIA	12/10/15	1/20/16	30
Diseño de Investigación	12/10/15	12/23/15	10
Tipo de Investigación	12/24/15	1/6/16	10
Población y muestra	1/7/16	1/20/16	10
RESULTADOS	1/21/16	3/23/16	45
Resultados	1/21/16	2/3/16	10
Propuesta técnica	2/4/16	2/24/16	15
Inversión de la propuesta	2/25/16	3/9/16	10
Cronograma de Actividades	3/10/16	3/23/16	10
CONCLUSIONES	3/24/16	4/6/16	10
REFERENCIAS BIBLIOGRAFICAS	4/7/16	4/20/16	10
ENTREGA	4/21/16	4/22/16	2
SUSTENTACION	4/25/16	4/25/16	1

Figure 37. Timeline of Activities.
Source: Own elaboration

VIII. BUDGET

The budget for this research project includes the following costs. The costs of the development of the business intelligence solution are divided into: Development costs of the business intelligence solution, overhead costs and other additional costs.

The expenses for services that include the services of the investigators, which amount to S/. 12,000.00 between both investigators.

General expenses include transport costs, stationery, printing, and other services such as electricity and internet, amounting to S/. 2,055.00. Adding the two groups of expenses together, they amount to S/. 14,055.00 (Fourteen thousand and fifty-five nuevos soles).

In addition, this project is 100% funded by the researchers.

PER DIEM AND ALLOWANCE ITEMS	ITEM	CANTI.	UNIT	COST UNIT.	PARTIAL COST
SERVICES-FEES	RESEARCH		GLOBAL	S/. 6000.00	S/. 12 000.00
TRANSPORT	MOBILITY		DIAS	S/. 5.00	S/. 100.00
EXPENDITURE	MEETINGS		UNIT	S/. 15.00	S/. 150.00
IMPRESSIONS	DOCUMENTS		MILLAR	S/. 500	S/. 1 000.00
	THESIS PLAN		EXEMPLAR	S/. 10.00	S/. 30.00
OTHER	ELECTRICITY	5	MONTHS	S/. 70.00	S/. 350.00
	INTERNET	5	MONTHS	S/. 85.00	S/. 425.00
				TOTAL INVESTMENT.	S/. 14 055.00

IX   ANNEXES

ANNEX 01.
Publication of the DataWareHouse - Dw

Step 01: Cube ready to publish

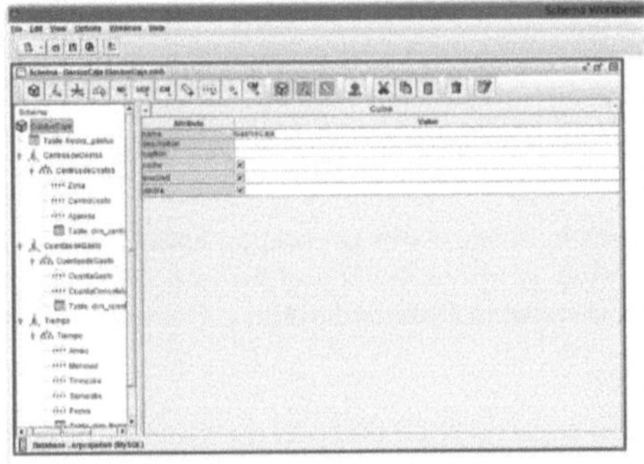

Step 02: Publishing the Cube - OLAP

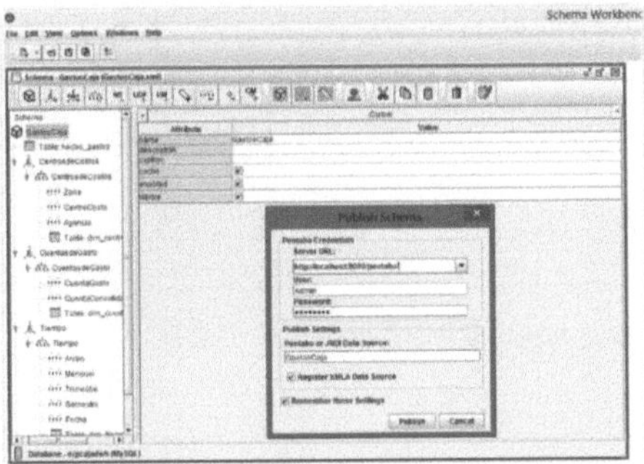

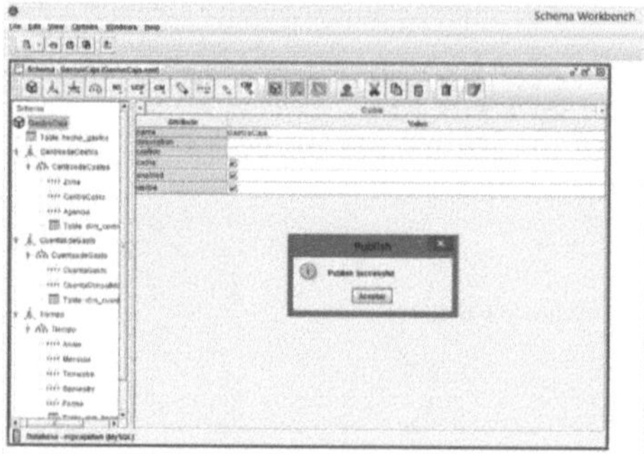

Step 03: After publishing the cube in Schema Workbench, go to the Pentaho BI server, and in the Connection option, generate its connection with the Dw base, to be able to see the cube already operative in Pivot or Sayku.
Right click, New connection.

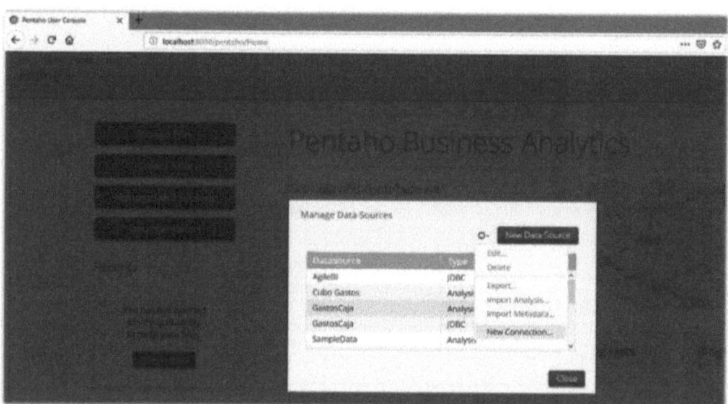

Step 04: The connection is then validated.

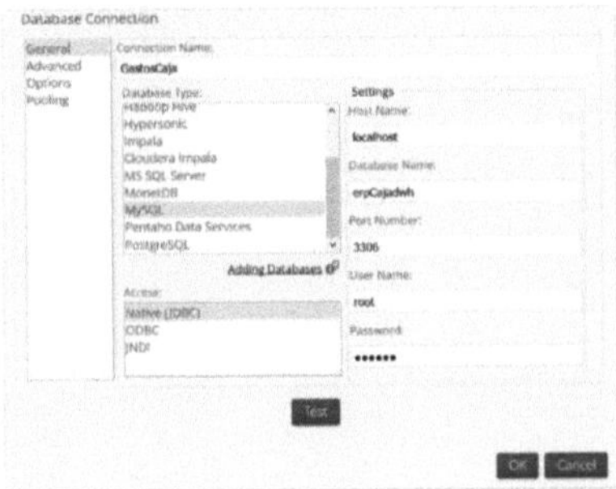

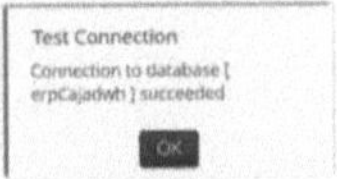

We should have, as an answer Satisfactory connection.

Steps 05: Presentation of the Results, we proceed to raise the Pentaho Server, with its user and password, to be able to show the Data.

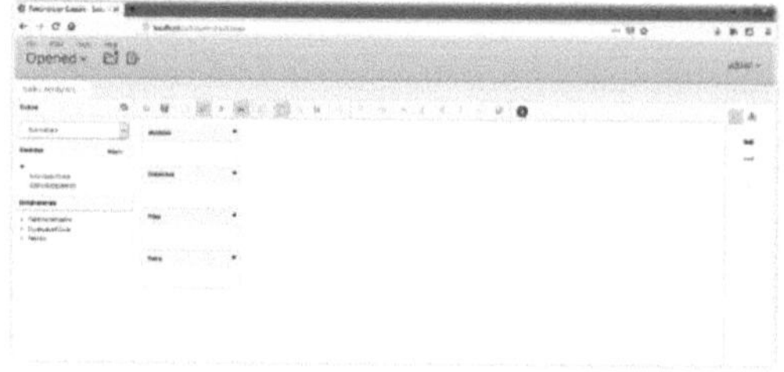

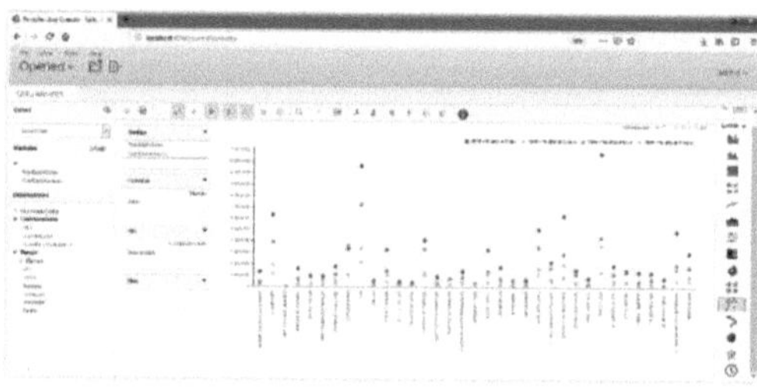

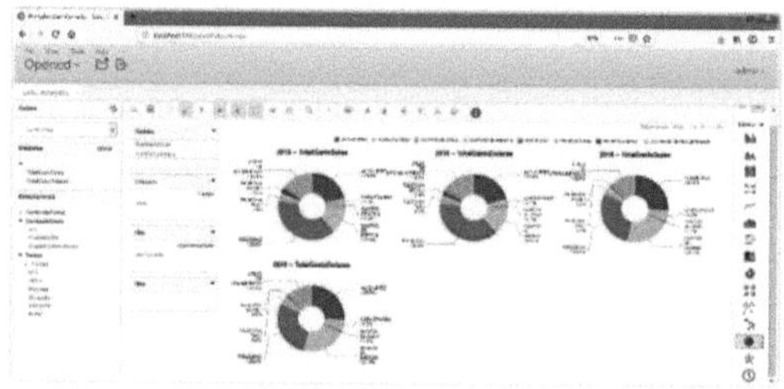

I want morebooks!

Buy your books fast and straightforward online - at one of world's fastest growing online book stores! Environmentally sound due to Print-on-Demand technologies.

Buy your books online at
www.morebooks.shop

Kaufen Sie Ihre Bücher schnell und unkompliziert online – auf einer der am schnellsten wachsenden Buchhandelsplattformen weltweit! Dank Print-On-Demand umwelt- und ressourcenschonend produziert.

Bücher schneller online kaufen
www.morebooks.shop

KS OmniScriptum Publishing
Brivibas gatve 197
LV-1039 Riga, Latvia
Telefax: +371 686 204 55

info@omniscriptum.com
www.omniscriptum.com

Printed by Books on Demand GmbH, Norderstedt / Germany